Sullivan's Music Trivia

The Greatest Music Trivia Book Ever...

Printed and bound in Great Britain by MPG Books Ltd, Bodmin

Distributed in the US by Publishers Group West

Arcane is an imprint of Sanctuary Publishing Limited
Sanctuary House, 45–53 Sinclair Road
London W14 0NS, United Kingdom

www.sanctuarypublishing.com

Reprinted 2003 (twice), 2004

Jacket artwork: Caroline Church
Jacket design: Splashdown

ISBN: 1-86074-511-3

Sullivan's Music Trivia

The Greatest Music Trivia Book Ever...

Paul Sullivan

arcane

This book is dedicated to my father, Michael Sullivan, one of those rare men who never lost his head over music, but who was always partial to a bit of Tom Jones and Frank Sinatra; and to my mother, Sylvia Sharp, the most ardent Elvis Presley aficionado the south of England has ever seen.

— ACKNOWLEDGEMENTS —

Thanks first of all to Iain MacGregor, Chris Harvey and the rest of the Sanctuary team for giving me the opportunity to take on this dream job. Massive thanks also to the following people, who devoted their precious time and energy to help research and authenticate the contents of this book:

Meegan Daly, Robert A Ditcher, Jonas Adam Divine, Julie Drazen, Shailja Dubé, Alyson Emory, Rudy Grahn, Jason Hait, Chris Johnson, Chris Karmiol, J Douglas Kerrigan, Stephen T McKnight, Nik Metcalf, Brian Mistretta, Gabrielle Moss, Alice Pryke, Leigh Anne Rehkopf, Julie Seabaugh, Zachary Paris, Jeff Zilahy.

— ABOUT THE AUTHOR —

Writer/photographer Paul Sullivan has been covering music, travel and culture for the last five years. His articles, features and photographs have appeared in a range of respected newspapers, magazines and internet publications such as *The Face*, *The Independent*, *The Wire*, *Dazed And Confused*, *Sleazenation*, *Muzik*, *DJ*, *Xlr8r*, *7*, *Dotmusic*, *Amazon*, *IDJ*, *Hip-Hop Connection*, *Knowledge*, *Touch* and *Urb*.

Sullivan's work has taken him all over the world, covering music scenes and cultural movements in places such as South Africa, Cuba, Brazil, Southeast Asia, North America, New Zealand, Australia and Europe.

He currently lives and works from London, though his insatiable wanderlust and passion for exploring new cultures and music prevents him from staying in one spot for too long...

— PREFACE —

All nations, societies and communities on our merry planet indulge in some kind of music and dance ritual – often a multitude of them. Throughout the 20th century especially, technology and globalisation have made the music of many of these cultures readily available to us.

Yet despite the incredible choice of music available to us today, the world of music trivia has habitually zoned in on the genres of rock and pop. This book will doubtless provide fuel for lovers of the pub quiz, but aims to extend beyond genre, era and culture: to dive more deeply into the vast ocean of sound that constantly surrounds us, yet of which we are often unaware.

Thus, the reader will encounter fascinating factoids and entertaining vignettes about music, instruments and dances ancient and new, mainstream and esoteric, urban and folk.

There is no overriding structure. The book is part compendium, part reference, part encyclopedia, part trivia collection and is intended to raise eyebrows, provoke thoughts, inspire research, generate smiles, start (and stop) conversations and perhaps even – weather permitting – arouse some passion.

It can be enjoyed alone or with friends, in the bathroom or in a bar, with or without a frozen margarita. Most importantly, though, the book should be approached with an open mind, an insatiable lust for all kinds of music and a bit of spare cash to enhance your record collection.

— CD STATS —

- The theoretical lifespan of a CD-R is around 100 years.
- The diameter of a CD is 12cm.
- CDs were developed by Philips and Sony and released in 1982.
- The first commercial CD album was Billy Joel's *52nd Street*, which was released in Japan in October 1982.
- Stretched out in a straight line, all the data stored on a CD would be over four miles long.
- The first CD single was Dire Straits' *Brothers In Arms*, manufactured in 1985 and released for promotional purposes in Germany to commemorate the band's 1985 European tour.
- A CD contains the equivalent of seven Zip disks of information, or 473 3.5" diskettes, or 400,000 pages of typed paper.
- Around 1/3 of recorded CDs are pirated.
- The number of recorded CDs and blank CDs sold has been about equal.

— LINE-UP OF THE FIRST GLASTONBURY FESTIVAL — (AKA PILTON FESTIVAL)

Inspired by a visit to a nearby Blues Festival, farmer Michael Eaves decided to throw a party of his own on his farm in Somerset, England. In September 1970 he held the first Pilton Festival, which would later become the Glastonbury Festival, the largest festival in Europe with an annual audience of up to 150,000 people. The original headliners of the 1970 event were to be The Kinks, but they pulled out. T Rex took their place.

Line-up: Marc Bolan And T-Rex, Al Stewart, Quintessence, The Amazing Blondel, Sam Apple Pie, Steamhammer, Ian Anderson, Duster Bennet, Keith Christmas and a smattering of local blues and folk bands.

— MOUTH MUSIC —

Traditionally known as *puirt-a-beul* (tunes of the mouth), mouth music is a Gaelic tradition of a cappella song (ie without musical accompaniment) that uses tongue-twisting, meaningless Gaelic words chosen purely for the rhythmical sounds they create. According to legend, the style originated in Scotland after a 1745 uprising when instruments were banned. Mouth music – also known as 'diddling' or 'lilting' – was sung for entertainment and at work places. A similar rhythmic style can be found in many musical cultures, such as scat singing in American jazz, West African call-and-response, and the Cajun style *reel à bouche* (mouth reel), which spawned from poverty and a lack of musical instruments to play.

— TYPES OF CHRISTIAN CHANT —

Ambrosian Chant
Gallican Chant
Gregorian Chant
Mozarabic Chant
Old Roman Chant
Sarum Chant
Armenian Chant
Byzantine Chant
Coptic Chant
Ethiopian Chant
Russian Chant
Syrian Chant

— JAPANESE TAIKO DRUMMING —

The drums used in Taiko (the word literally means 'big drum') can be up to 15 feet in diameter and weigh over 800lbs. An ancient Japanese art, Taiko is believed to have begun as an intimidation tool on battlefields and also used as a deterrent for evil spirits. The bellicose sound the drums create allegedly awakened the spirit of rain, and were usually played in celebration of a plentiful harvest. The drums are often carved from trees that are up to 200 years old. Since World War II, Taiko drumming has undergone a dramatic resurgence, and there are currently between 4,000 and 8,000 Taiko groups in Japan.

— SCHENKER'S DEEP STRUCTURE —

German pianist Heinrich Schenker believed that all tonal music could be understood at three different levels. His theory applied to the underlying structure of most composition and, although (deeply) controversial, has become popular as a means of understanding tonal music. Schenker's Deep Structure theory states that the simplest and most complex of songs can be reduced down to the following basic components:

Foreground – surface sounds, or the music as it is played

Middleground – the middleground layers that are progressively further from the surface.

Background – the most basic level of the music, far beneath the surface; based upon a few simple progressions that are the foundation of the entire work.

— CELESTIAL MUSICIANS —

Apollo (**aka Loxias**) – Greek god of music and prophecy.

Euterpe – One of the nine muses of Apollo; the muse of music.

Pan – Minor god of music, depicted playing reed pipes whose sound caused panic (hence the name).

Orpheus – Son of Calliope and the greatest musician and poet of Greek myth.

Ihy – Egyptian god of music and dancing.

Macuilxochitl – Aztec god of music.

Kulitta – Hittite goddess of music who serves Ishtar.

Ninatta – Another Hittite goddess of music who serves Ishtar.

Benten – Japanese goddess of love, eloquence, wisdom, the arts, music, knowledge, good fortune and water.

Dana O'Shee – Small, graceful and eternally young creatures of Irish folklore. A person enchanted by their music is forever lost.

Bes – Egyptian dwarf god of music for the common people, protector of children and women in labour.

Kendatsuba – Shinto and Buddhist god of music, medicine and children. Originally from Indian and Hindu mythology.

— MP3 STATS —

- An average CD song, three minutes long, takes up 32MB of space. A three-minute MP3 song takes up about 1.6MB. Approximately 20 MP3 songs can fit into the same space as one CD song.
- MP3 is an abbreviation for Moving Pictures Experts Group (MPEG) Layer-3. The Moving Pictures Experts Group (MPEG) was created in 1988.
- The first portable MP3 player was the MPMan from Saehan.
- The size of a typical MP3 audio track is around 4MB.

- MP3 was originally developed for high-quality digital film audio soundtracks, but was adapted by the market as a method of compressing all types of audio.
- In high-quality compression mode, MP3 compresses PCM audio by 11 times
- German company Fraunhofer Gesellschaft originally developed the algorithm used in MP3 in 1987. They patented the technology in Germany in 1989, and in the United States in 1996.
- MP3 is part of the video format MPEG-2. There is no MPEG-3. The key features of the planned MPEG-3 format were integrated into MPEG-2. The latest generation is MPEG-4.
- MP3.com was founded by Michael Robertson in November 1997 and is the largest MP3 site on the Internet, featuring over 562,000 songs by over 87,700 artists.
- Analysts report that just one of the many peer-to-peer file-sharing systems in operation is responsible for over 1.8 billion unauthorised downloads per month.
- In a recent survey of music consumers, 23 per cent said they are not buying more music because they are downloading or copying their music for free.

**Artists officially against downloading MP3s for free include: Metallica, Martine McBride, Brooks And Dunn, Vince Gill, The Dixie Chicks, Nelly, Missy Elliot, Stevie Wonder, Eve, DMX, Shakira, Britney Spears, P Diddy, Mary J Blige, Vanessa Carlton, Glen Ballard (producer), Luciano Pavarotti, Barenaked Ladies, Mandy Moore, John Rzeznik (The Goo Goo Dolls), Mark Knopfler (Dire Straits), Damon Dash, Stephan Jenkins (Third Eye Blind), Dr Dre.*

— BOTTLENECK —

The method of moving a bottleneck up and down a guitar fretboard to produce the trademark 'slide' blues sound is thought to have originated with legendary blues performer Son House, who experimented with sounds created by medicine bottles. However, others argue that it goes back to the trademark slide sound of Hawaiian guitar, which in turn can be traced back to the 1890s, when Hawaiian schoolboy Joseph Kekuku applied a discarded bolt to his Portuguese guitar. Today a metal finger cover is generally used instead of an actual bottle, though the likes of Missisipi Fred McDowell and Muddy Waters still use real bottles.

— CLASSIC SYNTH MANUFACTURERS —

ARP Instruments
Akai
Casio
Electronic Music Studios
E-mu
Ensoniq
Fairlight
Korg
Kurzweil
Moog
New England Digital
Oberheim
Roland Corporation
Sequential Circuits
Waldorf
Yamaha

— SPANDA —

Spanda is a Sanskrit term for the subtle creative pulse of the universe as it manifests into the dynamism (manifestation of force) of the living form. Within the practice of Kashmir Shaivism, a collection of 51 verses dating to the ninth-century collection, the Spanda (or Yoga of Vibration and Divine Pulsation) is believed to help those who can perceive it to gain a vision of unity-consciousness. To the Yogi alert enough to perceive this sound pulsating through the universe, the vibration is said to reveal that all energy is only an offshoot of spiritual energy.

— THE WORKINGS OF THE EAR —

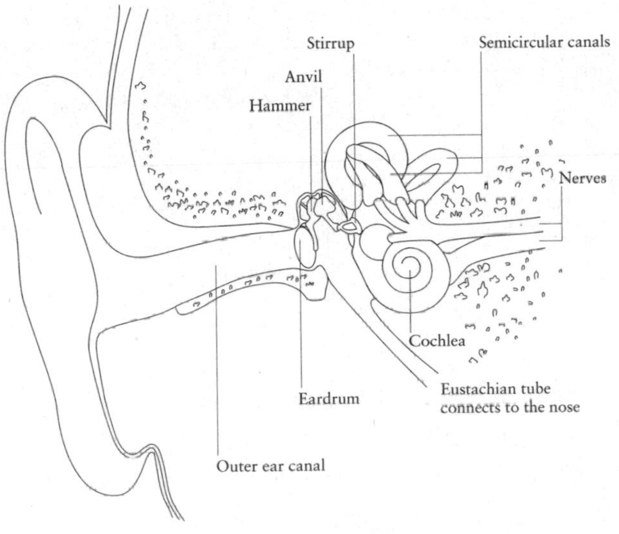

— BLUE NOTE —

The term 'blue note', usually associated with the famous jazz record label and New York club, in fact refers to the diminished fifth – the basic building-block chord of the blues.

— CHAT NOIR —

Established by artist Rodolphe Salis, *Le Chat Noir* ('The Black Cat') was the first musical cabaret in France. It was named after a mythical French cat who mocked the platitudes of the bourgeoisie and opened its doors in November 1881. The venue's early success was largely due to the mixing of piano music with free verse and poetry, an activity that was prohibited in France at the time. For many, Le Chat Noir encapsulated the tradition of mocking the establishment and its values through its rowdy and often profane activities.

— KINGS OF CALYPSO —

Calypso, the popular music of Trinidad, stems from the older kalinda, a ceremonial duel between two opponents accompanied by percussion and singing. Calypso often stresses political or social themes within the lyrics. Calypso King is a title normally given to the best performer at the annual carnival in Trinidad, but the following are simply legendary Calypso entertainers:

Atilla The Hun
Lord Invader
Lord Melody
King Radio
The Mighty Sparrow
Harry Belafonte
Lord Shorty

— WATER MUSIC —

Most toilets flush in E flat.

— HI-FIDELITY —

High-fidelity – aka 'hi-fi' – recording began in Germany during World War II. The Reichs-Rundfunk-Gesellschaft (German radio) produced experimental stereo-FM music broadcasts in Berlin in around 1941 using a customised magnetophone (tape machine), the AC-bias German tape recorder developed by engineers Weber and Von Braunmuhl for German electronics company AEG. When electrical engineer Jack Mullin was asked by the Allied Forces at the end of the war to investigate German recording technology, he discovered the incredible recording quality of the machine and, after improving the design, introduced it to the rest of the world. Today the term hi-fidelity, or hi-fi, has come to mean high-quality reproduction of sound and image that is particularly faithful to the original and is low in noticeable noise and distortion.

— SELECTED GUITAR MANUFACTURERS —

Leo Fender
Orville H Gibson
Freidrich Gretsch
August and Carl Larson
The CF Martin
Semie Moseley
John Dopyera
The Regal Musical Instrument Company
Adolph Rickenbacker
Selmer of Paris
Oscar Schmidt
Charles Stromberg
Washburn

— THE SINGING ARC OF WILLIAM DU BOIS DUDDELL — (1869–1942)

British physicist William Duddell was appointed in 1899 to solve the problem of noisy street lighting in London. The constant humming noise, he discovered, was generated from an arc that provided the light by creating a spark between two carbon nodes. During his troubleshooting experiments, Duddell found that if he varied the voltage supplied to the lamps he could create controllable audible frequencies. Attaching a keyboard to the arc lamps, he created one of the first electronic instruments and the first electronic instrument that was audible without using the telephone system as an amplifier/speaker. While exhibiting his invention to the London Institution of Electrical Engineers, it was noticed that arc lamps on the same circuit in other buildings also played music from Duddell's machine, thus inspiring the notion that music could be delivered over a lighting network. However, Duddell didn't capitalise on his discovery, nor did he file a patent for his instrument. Despite the important, visionary ramifications of his invention, and even though he embarked on a tour to show it off, the Singing Arc system never became more than a novelty.

— FAMOUS BOLLYWOOD SINGERS —

Lata Mangeshkar*
Asha Bhosle
Kavita Krishnamurthy Subramaniam
Udit Narayan
Kumar Sanu**
Alka Yagnik
Chitra
Sukhwinder Singh
Jaspinder Narula
Vasundhara Das

* *Lata Mangeshkar holds the Guinness world record for the number of songs recorded by one artist – over 50,000 at the last count.*

** *Kumar Sanu also holds a place in the* Guinness Book Of World Records *for having recorded the greatest number of songs in one day: 28.*

— BENJAMIN FRANKLIN AND HIS GLASS ARMONICA —

Scientist, humourist, statesman, inventor, musician, philosopher and economist Benjamin Franklin (1706–1790) made his mark in the world of music with the invention of the glass armonica in 1762. Whilst in England in 1757, he attended a concert given using wine glasses. This inspired him to create an instrument that would add harmonies to the delicate glass melodies. Franklin's instrument comprised different-sized bowls with holes and corks in the centre set onto a horizontal spindle, which was rotated by a flywheel and a foot pedal. The instrument was played by rubbing the edges of the bowls with moistened fingers, and it became popular throughout Europe: Marie Antoinette took lessons on it; Dr Mesmer (the famous hypnotist who gave his name to his art) put his patients into trances with it; and musical luminaries such as Mozart, Beethoven, Donizetti, Richard Strauss and Saint-Saëns composed for it.

— SONGS THAT SPELLED IT OUT —

'R.E.S.P.E.C.T.' – Aretha Franklin
'D.I.V.O.R.C.E.' – Tammy Wynette
'D.I.S.C.O.' – Ottowan
'P.Y.T.' (Pretty Young Thing) – Michael Jackson

'O.P.P.' (Other People's Property) –
Naughty By Nature
'L.O.V.E.' – Nat 'King' Cole
'A.B.C. (Easy As 1-2-3)' – The Jackson Five
'R.U.O.K.' – 2 Unlimited
'A.E.I.O.U.' – Freez
'P.A.S.S.I.O.N.' – Rhythm Syndicate
'I.G.Y. (What A Beautiful World)' –
Donald Fagen
'H.E.L.P. Is On The Way' – The Beach Boys
'M.T.A.' – Hawes, Steiner
'B-A-B-Y' – Carla Thomas
'K-A-T-I-E (The Name Spelling Song)' –
Karl Williams
'M-O-T-H-E-R (A Word That Means The
World To Me)' – Howard Johnson
'F.E.E.L.I.N.G. C.A.L.L.E.D. L.O.V.E.' – Pulp
'Y.M.C.A.' – The Village People
'S.O.S.' – Abba

— FLATS AND SHARPS FOR EACH KEY — IN THE MAJOR SCALE

C – None
G – F♯
D – F♯, C♯
A – F♯, C♯, G♯
E – F♯, C♯, G♯, D♯
B – F♯, C♯, G♯, D♯, A♯
F♯ – F♯, C♯, G♯, D♯, A♯, E♯
G♭ – B♭, E♭, A♭, D♭, G♭
A♭ – B♭, E♭, A♭, D♭
E♭ – B♭, E♭, A♭
B♭ – B♭, E♭
F – B♭

— CHANGE RINGING —

Change Ringing, developed in England during the 1500s, evolving gradually away from continental bell-ringing methods. It involves bells being swung in a complete circle by a single person so that, the more bells there are, the more people there are – six bells for six people, etc. The essence of Change Ringing is ringing the bells in a precise relationship to one another. Rung in the order from the lightest, highest-pitched bell to the heaviest, the bells strike in a sequence known as *rounds*, which ringers denote by a row of numbers. In order to ring a different row with each pull of the rope, ringers have what are called *methods* – orderly systems of changing pairs. Methods are constantly changing and never-repeating patterns are learnt by heart by the ringers and named after their creators (eg. Stedman). The names are followed by the number of bells appropriate, such as the Stedman Doubles on Six Bells, or the Stedman Triples on Eight Bells.

Experienced ringers test and extend their abilities by ringing peals (5,000 or more changes without breaks or repeating a row). The first peal was rung in England in 1715.

- In 1643 Parliament passed an Act forbidding persons from being present at ringing of bells for pleasure.
- During wartime, bells are often melted down to make cannon. During peacetime, cannon are often melted down to make bells.
- The bell, book and candle are instruments used for exorcism, bells being the *Vox Domini*, or the Voice of God.

— THE BEST OF ANDREW LLOYD WEBBER —

Aspects Of Love
Phantom Of The Opera
Starlight Express 3D
Jesus Christ Superstar
Joseph And The Amazing Technicolour Dreamcoat
The Beautiful Game
Notting Hill
Cats
Evita
Gumshoe

— CAN-CAN —

Reports of dances involving high-kicking have been recorded since ancient times, but the style reached a notorious peak in the shape of the can-can during the late 19th century. Ostensibly a hybrid of the polka and the quadrille, the can-can (the word originally meant 'tittle-tattle of a scandalous nature') was originally a group dance performed by both sexes, but it eventually came to be dominated by women who wore exuberant costumes and showed the flesh above their stockings by kicking their legs high in the air. The dance was deemed immoral and indecent and was outlawed for a number of years, though it still managed to become popular through venues such as the Moulin Rouge, gaining extra respectability via French operetta composers.

— JEW'S HARP —

Known as a *gewgaw* in England, a *vargan* in Russia, a *maultrommel* in Germany and a *genggong* in Bali, the Jew's harp is neither Jewish nor a harp. It is a small instrument that consists of a metal hoop with a flexible metal reed (with an up-bent end) attached in the middle. The harp is held in front of the mouth while the player plucks the reed using his hand. While a Jew's harp can produce only one tone, the sound can be manipulated by using the throat, breath, tongue and lips. There is no universally accepted playing technique.

The instrument did not catch on in Europe until before the 13th century, when it gained popularity as a rural folk-music instrument, but interest had waned by the 19th century. In different cultures and at different times, the Jew's harp has been used by troubadours, shamen, clerics and entertainers.

— DALCROZE METHOD —

The Dalcroze method was created by Swiss music educator and composer Emile Jacques-Dalcroze (1865-1950) as a way of giving students a living experience of music. A system of co-ordinating the body with music, the method aims to promote alertness, expression and a sense of musical structure and phrasing via three main branches: eurhythmics, solfege and improvisation. Where eurythmics trains the body in musical skills such as rhythm and dynamics through kinetic exercises, solfege incorporates the skills learned through eurythmics, essentially training the eyes, ears and voice in melody, harmony and pitch, while improvisation combines the two branches above with the student's spontaneous creativity in movement and vocal and/or instrumental abilities. The three branches are not singular steps, but often overlapping, or interrelated. An essential feature of this method is the idea of 'feel first, then express'.

— ESSENTIAL DRUM TECHNIQUES —

- Single-Stroke Roll
- Single-Stroke Four
- Single-Stroke Seven
- Single Paradiddle
- Double Paradiddle
- Triple Paradiddle
- Paradiddle-diddle
- Ruff
- Single-Drag Tap
- Double-Drag Tap
- Lesson 25
- Drag Paradiddle #1
- Drag Paradiddle #2
- Single Ratamcue
- Double Ratamcue
- Triple Ratamcue
- Flamacue
- Swiss (Army) Triplet
- Pataflafla
- Ratatap
- Multiple Bounce Roll
- Triple-Stroke Roll
- Double-Stroke Roll
- Five-Stroke Roll
- Buzz Roll
- Six-Stroke Roll
- Seven-Stroke Roll
- Nine-Stroke Roll
- Ten-Stroke Roll
- Eleven-Stroke Roll
- Thirteen-Stroke Roll
- Fifteen-Stroke Roll
- Seventeen-Stroke Roll
- Flam
- Flam Accent
- Flam Tap
- Flamacue
- Flam Paradiddle
- Flam Paradiddle-diddle
- Flam Drag

— THE LARGEST COUNTRY LINE DANCE EVER —

On 29 January 2000 in Tamworth, Australia, 6,275 people danced to Brooks And Dunn's 'Bootscooting Boogie' for six minutes and 28 seconds.

— MEMBERS OF THE DULCIMER FAMILY —

Appalachian Mountain Dulcimer, USA
Bandura, Ukraine
Epinette des Vosges, France
Cimbaloms (Cymbalom), Hungry
Hackbräde, Sweden
Hackbrett, Germany/Austria/Switzerland
Hammered Dulcimer, USA
Hummel, Holland/Belgium
Quanoon, Egypt
Qanoun, Arabia (UAE)
Santir, Iran
Santur, Greece
Santoor, India
Tarn Thap Luc, Vietnam
Tiompán, Ireland
Tsambal, Romania
Tsimbl, Jewish
Yangum, Korea
Yang Quin (Or Yang Ch'in), China

— THE FURRY DANCE OF HELSTON, CORNWALL, UK —

One of the oldest surviving traditions in the UK, the Furry Dance of Helston, Cornwall, takes place on 8 May each year*. The dance consists primarily of a procession through the town (including homes, shops and gardens) where the men wear top hats and tails, the women sport their best dresses and hats, and children dress all in white. The dance stems from the pagan celebration of the beginning of spring and the end of winter and is planned to correspond with the feast of the archangel Michael.

**unless the date falls on a Sunday or Monday, in which case it is celebrated on the previous Saturday*

— HOW TO DO THE HIGHLAND FLING (STEP BY STEP) —

- Hold the left arm up and curve towards the top of the head to create a 'C'.
- Put the right hand on the hip with the thumb pointing towards the ground and the fingers towards the back.
- Starting on the left foot, with the right foot extended to the right-hand side, take a quarter-turn hop (while essentially remaining in the same spot).
- Bring the right foot in behind the right ankle.
- Perform another quarter-turn hop on the left foot, again extending the right foot out to the right-hand side.
- Then another quarter-turn hop, bringing the right foot in front of the left calf with the toe pointing down.
- Repeat the previous steps but with arms and legs in the opposite positions.
- End the dance with a slow and elegant bow.

— HARMOLODIC MELODY —

The phrase 'harmolodic melody' was coined by free-jazz musician Ornette Coleman in the '60s. More a philosophy of life than a coherent musical theory, the concept was never delivered with any great clarity. Some believe that the phrase is derived from the words harmony, movement and melody. Others state that the term refers to the harmonies established when the same melodic line is played in different keys, pitches and intonations simultaneously but otherwise left unaltered. Yet another interpretation implies that all instruments are of equal import and that accordingly there should be no separation between soloist and accompanying instruments.

THE *EXEQUIE* MIXTAPE — (MUSIC TO HAVE A CATHOLIC FUNERAL RITE TO) —

'All Creatures Of Our God And King'
'Alleluia! Sing To Jesus'
'Amazing Grace'
'Crown Him With Many Crowns'
'For All The Saints'
'Holy God, We Praise Thy Name'
'I Know That My Redeemer Lives'
'Lord Of All Hopefulness'
'Be Not Afraid'
'To Jesus Christ, Our Sovereign King'
'On Eagle's Wings'
'Here I Am, Lord'
'Sing With All The Saints In Glory'
'O God, Our Help In Ages Past'
'I Am The Bread Of Life'
'Taste And See'
'Song Of Farewell'
'In Paradisum'
'Panis Angelicus'

— THE OXFORD BOOK OF CAROLS (1928) —

The Oxford Book Of Carols was responsible for the popularisation of many now-famous Christmas carols, such as...

'God Rest Ye, Merry Gentleman'
'The First Noel'
'Good King Wenceslas'
'In Terra Pax'
'Hail Mary, Full of Grace'
'Hark, The Herald Angels Sing'
'Three Kings of Orient'
'The 12 Days Of Christmas'
'We Wish You A Merry Christmas'

— THE 'CATALOGUE' ARIA —

The 'Catalogue' aria is the nickname given to Leporello's aria in Act 1, Scene 2 of Mozart's *Don Giovanni*, in which he recounts a list of Don Giovanni's sexual conquests. They are...

Italy – 640
Germany – 231
France – 100
Turkey – 91
Spain – 1,003

Total – 2,065

— TAILGATE TROMBONE —

Tailgates – where the trombone plays a rhythmic line underneath trumpets and cornets – take their name from New Orleans funeral processions. The tradition was for brass bands to be transported on trucks through the streets. The tailgates of these vehicles were lowered to allow trombonists freedom of movement for their slides.

— THE WORLD'S LARGEST PIPE ORGAN —

The Convention Hall organ in Atlantic City, New Jersey, is officially the world's largest pipe organ. When completed (between May 1929 and December 1932 by the Midmer–Losh Organ Company of Merrick, Long Island, New York), it boasted two consoles (one with seven manuals and another moveable one with five), more than 1,000 stop controls and over 33,000 pipes which ranged in length from 0.2ft to 64ft. The instrument is also the loudest musical instrument ever constructed and is allegdly able to match the volume of 25 brass bands. The loudest stop, the Grand Ophicleide (16ft and 8ft), is believed to be more than six times the volume of the loudest locomotive whistle.

— LONGEST RUNNING WEST END MUSICALS —

Cats – 11 May 1981–11 May 2002 (21 years)

Starlight Express – 12 March 1984–12 January 2002 (17 years)

Les Miserables – 4 December 1985 (still running – 17 years and counting)

Phantom Of The Opera – 10 September 1986 (still running – 16 years and counting)

Blood Brothers – 21 November 1991 (still running – 11 years and counting)

* The Fantasticks *is the world's longest running musical, opening in May 1960 and closing in January 2002, nearly 42 years later.*

— LONG PLAYING RECORD —

Pink Floyd's *The Dark Side Of The Moon* stayed on the *Billboard* Top 200 album charts for 591 consecutive weeks – 11.4 years. The LP has moved in and out of the Top 200 for an incredible 741 weeks (14 years) and has spent 26 years on various other *Billboard* charts.

* *When the album hit Number One for just one week in 1973, David Gilmour won his bet with manager Steve O'Rourke that the album wouldn't crack the US Top Ten.*

** *At Pink Floyd's outdoor concert at London's Crystal Palace Bowl in 1970, they played so loud that most of the fish in the lake in front of the natural amphitheatre's stage were killed.*

— HOW TO PLAY THE GONG (STEP BY STEP) —

- Warm up the gong by hitting it gently outside the centre, preferably with a leather- or felt-covered mallet.
- When the gong is vibrating slightly, smack it hard in the centre.
- Allow the gong's ring to get softer and softer until it eventually stops.
- Smack the gong again in the centre.
- Repeat process.

— A TIMELINE OF TAPDANCERS —

1850 1900 1950 2000

John Diamond
Henry 'Juba' Lane
George Primrose (Delaney)
Bill 'Bo Jangles' Robinson
King Rastus Brown
Willie Covan
Fred Astaire
John (Sublett) Bubbles
George Murphy
Clayton 'Peg Leg' Bates
Mae Barnes
Leonard Reed
Buddy and Vilma Ebsen
Paul Draper
Maceo Anderson
Ruby Keeler
Hermes Pan
Honi Coles
Bubba Gaines
Gene Kelly
Dorothy/Paul Toy/Wing
Charles 'Cholly' Atkins
Ralph Brown
Stan Kahn
Fred Kelly
Jeni LeGon
Prince Spencer
Eddie Brown
Steve Condos
Frances Nealy
Fayard Nicholas
Charles 'Chuck' Green
Flash McDonald
Gene Nelson
Baby Laurence
Warren Berry
Bunny Briggs
Leon Collins
Ann Miller
Harold Nicholas
Peggy Ryan
Donald O'Connor
Jane Withers
Lon Chaney
LaVaughn Robinson
Shirley Temple
Jimmy Slyde
Harriet Browne
Brenda Bufalino

— FASHION LINES BY SINGERS AND RAPPERS —

Sean 'Puffy/P Diddy' Combs – Sean John
Britney Spears – Britney Jeans
Jay-Z – Roc-A-Wear
Chris Kirkpatrick – Fuman Skeeto
Lil' Kim – Queen Beetique Monkees/Zilch
Eminem – Shady Gear
Mike D (The Beastie Boys) – X-Large
Master P – No Limit (clothing, toys and even pre-paid phone cards)
Wu-Tang Clan – Wu-Wear
Sisqo – Dragon
Busta Rhymes – Bushi Designs
Russell Simmons (Def Jam co-founder) – Phat Farm
Naughty By Nature – Naughty Gear
Snoop Dogg – Snoop Dogg
Outkast – Outkast
Jennifer Lopez – J-Lo

— FAMOUS DANCE PIECES BY MARTHA GRAHAM —

Dancer and choreographer Martha Graham (1894–1991) is one of the central figures of the modern dance movement. Throughout her 50-year-long career, Graham created more than 180 works and developed an original technique that involved the expression of primal emotions through stylised bodily movement of great intensity.

El Penitente (1940)
Letter To The World (1940)
Deaths And Entrances (1943)
Hérodiade (1944)
Appalachian Spring (1944)
Cave Of The Heart (1946)
Errand Into The Maze (1947)
Night Journey (1947)
Judith (1950)
Seraphic Dialogue (1955)
Clytemnestra (1958)
Embattled Garden (1958)
Episodes: Part 1 (1959)
Alcestis (1960)
Phaedra (1962)

FAMOUS DANCE PIECES — BY MARTHA GRAHAM (CONTINUED) —

Circe (1963)
The Witch Of Endor (1965)
A Time Of Snow (1968)
Mendicants Of Evening (1973)
Myth Of A Voyage (1973)
Holy Jungle (1974)
Lucifer (1975)
Ecuatorial (1978)
The Owl And The Pussycat (1978)
Acts Of Light (1981)
The Rite Of Spring (1984)
Persephone (1987)
Maple-Leaf Rag (1990)

— THE MELLOTRON —

The Mellotron is often referred to as the world's first sampler. It is a unique machine, filled with spools of magnetic tape, enabling it to emit a pre-recorded sound when a key is pressed down. Each key has its own tapehead and motor, which can engage a length of tape and 'play' the sound. The Mellotron can also produce regular instrumental sounds as well as sound effects, depending on the tapes loaded, and became popular with various '60s and '70s bands like Yes, Genesis, Led Zeppelin, The Kinks, The Rolling Stones and The Beatles.

- The Mellotron was invented by Harry Chamberlin in 1946.
- Mellotrons are all based on the principle that each key sets a length of tape in motion, thus playing back whatever was recorded on the tape.
- The first Mellotron was the Mellotron Mark 1.
- The smallest Mellotron weighed approximately 122lbs.
- The most popular Mellotron sold 1,800 units.
- The Mellotron's big advantages over other synthesisers was its polyphony and the high quality of the sounds.
- The Mellotron eventually disappeared due to it's weight and bulk and its inability to match the capacities of the modern sampler.
- The last Mellotron was made in 1986.

— V DISCS —

On 31 July 1942, the American Federation of Musicians (headed by James C Petrillo) went on strike to seek royalties from record companies. As it was wartime, the strike cut off the supply of new recordings to the troops overseas. Sound engineer and army lieutenant Robert Vincent approached the War Department with the idea of recording music especially for the troops and received approval from Washington in July 1943. He helped develop the V-disc programme, for which all fees and royalties from recording companies and unions – including the striking AFM – were waived in exchange for the army's assurance that the unions that V-discs would be for the use of military personnel only and would not be available commercially. The first V-discs were shipped on 1 October 1943 from the RCA Victor pressing plant in Camden, New Jersey. V-discs were larger than commercial 78rpm records – 12" instead of 10" – and were often cut with up to 136 grooves per inch They allowed six minutes of music at a time when the standard commercial disc was limited to less than four minutes per side. Production of V-discs lasted for six years in total, with 900 unique discs being created – containing 3,000 separate recordings – more than eight million of which were shipped overseas.

V-disc artists included: Dinah Shore, Bing Crosby, Lena Horne, Ginny Simms, Jo Stafford, Nat 'King' Cole, Louis Prima, Dick Haymes, Perry Como, Frank Sinatra, The Mills Brothers, The Andrews Sisters, Johnny Mercer, Jack Teagarden, Artie Shaw, Buddy Rich, Les Paul, Glenn Miller, Guy Lombardo, Louis Armstrong, Count Basie, Louis Jordan, Tommy Dorsey, Ella Fitzgerald, Paul Robeson, Abbot And Costello, Roy Eldridge, Art Tatum, Spike Jones, Fats Waller, Cab Calloway, Bob Wills, Bill Boyd, Roy Acuff.

— HOOVER'S HARPIST —

The first artist to play at the White House for a Head of State was harpist Mildred Dilling, on 29 April 1931. She was invited by J Edgar Hoover to play for King Phra Pok Klao Prajadhipok of Siam. The tradition continues to this day.

FRANKLIN D ROOSEVELT'S LETTER — TO THE PRESIDENT OF THE NATIONAL — FEDERATION OF MUSIC CLUBS (1941)

'The inspiration of great music can help to inspire a fervour for the spiritual values in our way of life; and thus to strengthen democracy against those forces which would subjugate and enthrall mankind. Because music knows no barriers of languages, because it recognises no impediments to free intercommunication, because it speaks a universal tongue, music can make us all more vividly aware of that common humanity which is ours and which shall one day unite the nations of the world in one great brotherhood.'

— TOP-SELLING ALBUMS IN THE UK —

Sergeant Pepper's Lonely Hearts Club Band – The Beatles (1967)

(What's The Story) Morning Glory – Oasis (1995)

Bad – Michael Jackson (1987)

Brothers In Arms – Dire Straits (1985)

Stars – Simply Red (1991)

Thriller – Michael Jackson (1982)

Greatest Hits (Volume One) – Queen (1981)

Spice – The Spice Girls (1996)

Abba Gold – Greatest Hits – Abba (1990)

The Immaculate Collection – Madonna (1990)

— THE VILLAGE PEOPLE —

*Formed 1977 in Greenwich Village, NYC.

Alex Briley (Military Man/Sailor)
David Hodo (Construction Worker)
Glenn Hughes (Leatherman/Biker)
Eric Anzalone (Leatherman/Biker)
Jeff Olson (Cowboy)
Felipe Rose (Indian)
Ray Simpson (Policeman/Frontman)
Victor Willis (Policeman/Frontman)
Randy Jones (Cowboy)

— A BRIEF HISTORY OF CHIME —

The Westminster Chimes were originally called the Cambridge Chimes, due to their being fitted initially to the clock of the university church of St Mary's the Great in Cambridge, England. The famous tune E-D-C-G is derived from Handel's oratorio *The Messiah* (a piece written by Cambridge organ student William Crotch in 1793) and was first broadcast by the BBC in 1923. The original words to the tune are 'Lord, through this be thou our guide so, by thy power, no foot shall slide'. The bells are tuned to the key of F major with the hour bell (Big Ben) sounding E.

— THE BRISTOL SESSIONS —

In 1927 music producer Ralph Peer travelled to Bristol in the southern Appalachian region of the USA to find some fresh music and record it. He set up his new electrical recording equipment (made by Western Electric) on the second floor of the Taylor–Christian hat company's warehouse at 410 State Street and started his recording sessions with Ernest Stoneman and some of his friends on 25 July 1927. Peer eventually recorded The Carter Family and Jimmie Rodgers, making them the first commercially successful modern country-music artists and launching country music to the masses for the first time.

— THE ICE CREAM CODE —

According to the Ice Cream Van Chimes Code Of Practice (1982) you should not sound chimes...

- for longer than four seconds at a time
- more often than once every three minutes
- when the vehicle is stationary
- except on approach to a selling point
- when in sight of another ice-cream van which is trading
- when within 50m of schools (during school hours), hospitals, and places of worship (on Sundays and any other recognised days of worship)
- more often than once every two hours in the same street
- louder than 80dB at 7.5m
- as loudly in quiet areas or narrow streets as elsewhere

NAMES OF KEYS IN FRENCH, — GERMAN, ITALIAN AND SPANISH —

English	French	German	Italian	Spanish
major	majeur	Dur	maggiore	mayor
minor	mineur	Moll	minore	menor
sharp	dièse	-is	diesis	sostenido
flat	bémol	-es	bemolle	bemol

English	French	German	Italian	Spanish
A flat	la bémol	as	la bemolle	la bemol
A	la	A	la	La
A sharp	la dièse	ais	la diesis	la sostenido
B flat	si bémol	B	si bemolle	si bemol
B	si	H	si	Si
C flat	do bémol	ces	do bemolle	Do bemol
C	ut/do	C	do	Do
C sharp	do dièse	cis	do diesis	Do sostenido
D flat	ré bémol	des	re bemolle	Re bemol
D	ré	D	re	Re
D sharp	ré dièse	dis	re diesis	Re sostenido
E flat	mi bémol	es	mi bemolle	Mi bemol
E	mi	E	mi	Mi
F	fa	F	f	Fa
F sharp	fa dièse	fis	fa diesis	fa sostenido
G flat	sol bémol	ges	sol bemolle	sol bemol
G	sol	G	sol	sol
G sharp	sol dièse	gis	sol diesis	sol sostenido

— TEN SONGS BANNED BY THE BBC — FOR BEING TOO RAUNCHY

Jane Birkin And Serge Gainsbourg – 'Je T'aime (Moi Non Plus)' 1969
Frankie Goes To Hollywood – 'Relax' 1983
The Au Pairs – 'Come Again' 1981
Lil Louis – 'French Kiss' 1989
The Troggs – 'I Can't Control Myself' 1966
The Rolling Stones – 'Let's Spend The Night Together' 1967

The Stranglers – 'Peaches'	1977
Scott Walker – 'Jackie'	1967
George Michael – 'I Want Your Sex'	1987
Max Romeo – 'Wet Dream'	1969
Donna Summer – 'Love To Love You'	1976

— RASTA PATOIS —

Babylon: the system, establishment, police
Bad: good
Bafan: clumsy
Bambu: rolling papers
Bangarang: a fuss, an uproar
Bobo: an idiot
Cho: expression of impatience
Cris: fresh, crisp
Cuss-Cuss: a fight, an argument
Don Dada: top dog, highest of all dons
Downpressor: an oppressor
Dread: person with dreadlocks
Gravalicious: greedy, avaricious
Large: respected
Ranking: even more respected
Rass Clot: a curse
Rude Boy: a criminal, bad boy
Seen: I understand, I agree
Seen?: do you understand? do you agree?
Star: a friend, good guy
Vex: to stresss out
Yard: home

— DUENDE —

Duende is a word used in flamenco to describe the hypnotic fixation that one may experience while enjoying a flamenco performance. It equates roughly to a soul, or an inner spirit, which is released as a result of a performer's intense emotional involvement with the music, song and dance.

— FIRST PUBLISHED UK CHART — (14th NOVEMBER 1952)

Position	Title	Artist
1	'Here In My Heart'	Al Martino
2	'You Belong To Me'	Jo Stafford
3	'Somewhere Along The Way'	Nat 'King' Cole
4	'Isle Of Innisfree'	Bing Crosby
5	'Feet Up'	Guy Mitchell
6	'Half As Much'	Rosemary Clooney
7	'Forget Me Not'	Vera Lynn
7	'High Noon'	Frankie Laine
8	'Sugarbush'	Doris Day And Frankie Laine
8	'Blue Tango'	Ray Martin
9	'Homing Waltz'	Vera Lynn
10	'Auf Wiedersehen'	Vera Lynn
11	'Because You're Mine'	Mario Lanza
11	'Cowpuncher's Cantata'	Max Bygraves
12	'Walking My Baby Back Home'	Johnnie Ray

— THE MANY MONIKERS OF DUKE ELLINGTON —

The Washingtonians
Sonny And The Deacons
Zaidee Jackson With Lulu Belle's Boy Friends
Rex Stewart And His Fifty-Second Street Stompers
Barney Bigard And His Jazzopaters
Cootie Williams And His Rug-Cutters
Ivie Anderson And Her Boys From Dixie
Johnny Hodges And His Orchestra
Rex Stewart And His 52nd Street Stompers
Barney Bigard And His Orchestra
The Traymore Orchestra
Warren Mills And His Blue Serenaders
The Harlem Footwarmers
The Chicago Footwarmers
The Jungle Band
Joe Turner And His Memphis Men
Sonny Greer And His Harlem Hot Chocolates
The Harlem Music Masters
The Philadelphia Melodians

The Memphis Hot Shots
The Whoopie Makers
The Louisiana Rhythmakers
Earl Jackson And His Musical Champions
The New York Synchopators
Chick Winters And His Orchestra Dixie Jazz Band

— BRITISH PHONOGRAPHIC INSTITUTE (BPI) — CERTIFIED AWARDS

The BPI Awards were introduced in April 1973 in order to measure the performance of individual records based on sales. Qualification for albums was initially on the basis of revenue received by manufacturers, but from January 1978 the BPI council abolished the old monetary system for albums and replaced it with a unit system. The qualifying unit levels are as follows...

Albums		**Singles**	
Silver	60,000	Silver	200,000
Gold	100,000	Gold	400,000
Platinum	300,000	Platinum	600,000

— MOST VALUABLE MUSIC MANUSCRIPT —

The record payment for a music manuscript is $4.1 million, paid by James Kirkman in 1987 for a bound volume of symphonies in Mozart's handwriting.

— THE FIRST EVER RADIO BROADCAST —

On Christmas Eve 1906, Reginald Fessenden made history by broadcasting music and speech from Massachusetts. His broadcast was heard as far away as the West Indies. After picking it up, the United Fruit Company purchased equipment from Fessenden to communicate with its ships. During the broadcast, Fessenden played 'O Holy Night' on the violin and also played the first record to be played across the airwaves, Handel's 'Largo', making him the world's first DJ.

— LABANOTATION —

Labanotation is a system of notating human movement developed by Austro-Hungarian Rudolf von Laban (1879–1958). The shapes of the symbols tell you the direction of the movement. The symbol's position is placed on the staff tells you the part of the body that is to perform the movement, the shading of the symbol tells the intensity of the movement, and the length of the symbol indicates the length of duration of the movement.

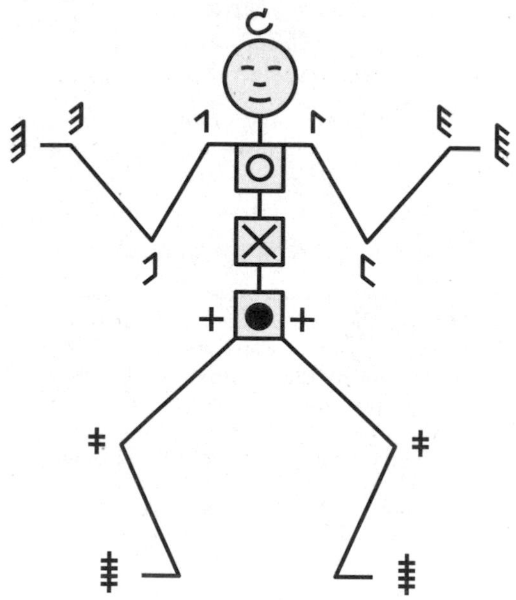

— TITLES OF ERIK SATIE WORKS —

Erik Satie was an eccentric and playful character whose compositions are regarded as forerunners to the Minimalist movement. He experimented with what he dubbed 'furniture music': music that was supposed to be in the background rather than listened to. Many of his compositions have influences from medieval music and from other French composers, and a great deal of them bore intriguing titles...

'To Be Jealous Of One's Playmate Who Has A Big Head'
'The War Song Of The King Of Beans'
'Canine Song'
'To Profit By The Corns On His Feet To Grab His Hoop'
'Indoors Voice'
'Veritable Flabby Preludes (For A Dog)'
'Sketches And Exasperations Of A Big Boob Made Of Wood'
'Five Grins, Or Mona Lisa's Moustache'
'Menus For Childish Purposes'
'Dessicated Embryos'
'A Skinny Dance'
'She Who Talks Too Much'
'Three Pieces In The Form Of A Pear'
'The Angora Ox'
'The Dreamy Fish'
'Five Grimaces'

— THE BEATLES' 'BUTCHER' COVER —

The original cover of the Beatle's album *Yesterday And Today* (1966) showed them dressed in white smocks, covered with raw meat and surrounded by baby dolls that had been decapitated. The photo was allegedly taken as a joke to give the band a break form all the recent publicity shots they had endured for 'Paperback Writer'. Capitol decided to use it as an official album shot, but when it ended up causing an outrage, they had to recall the albums and re-issue them with a less controversial photo. To save money, Capitol glued the new cover (which depicts the band looking slightly bored around an old beat-up suitcase) on top of many of the recalled albums, so many copies of the LP still have the original artwork underneath. The 'butcher cover' today is highly collectible.

— TEN THINGS YOU POSSIBLY DIDN'T KNOW — ABOUT…THE BEATLES

- John Lennon named his cat Jesus.
- The album *Please, Please Me* was recorded in less than ten hours.
- In 1962 the Beatles won a contest held by a Merseyside newspaper to see who was the biggest band in Liverpool. One of the main reasons why they won is because the band called in repeatedly, posing as different people and voting for themselves.
- John Lennon was the first cover star of *Rolling Stone* magazine, in 1967. He was also photographed for the cover of *Rolling Stone* on the day he was assassinated.
- In 2001 Liverpool Airport was renamed John Lennon Airport after him.
- At the end of 'A Day In The Life', an ultrasonic whistle audible only to dogs was recorded by Paul McCartney for his Shetland sheepdog.
- The *Sergeant Pepper's* album took four months and $75,000 (£50,000) to produce.
- During the final days of The Quarry Men (The Beatles' former band), John Lennon smashed Pete Shotton over the head with his own washboard. He later apologised by buying him a supermarket.
- George Harrison's mother answered all of his fan mail until 1968.
- When Paul McCartney married Linda Eastman in 1969, no other Beatle attended the wedding.

— TEN CLASSICS PENNED BY NORMAN WHITFIELD —

Marvin Gaye	'I Heard It Through The Grapevine'	Tamla	1968
Edwin Starr	'War'	Gordy	1970
Rose Royce	'Carwash'	MCA	1977
The Temptations	'Papa Was A Rolling Stone'	Gordy	1972
The Dave Clarke Five	'You Got What It Takes'	Epic	1967

Jackie Wilson	'I'll Be Satisfied'	Brunswick	1959
The Temptations	'Just My Imagination (Running Away With Me)'	Gordy	1971
The Undisputed Truth	'Smiling Faces Sometimes'	Gordy	1971
Jackson 5	'Get It Together'	Motown	1977
Rare Earth	'(I Know) I'm Losing You'	Rare Earth	1970

— THE FIRST ROCK 'N' ROLL STAR TO BE MADE — INTO A WAXWORK AT MADAME TUSSAUD'S

Tommy Steele

— HAPPY BIRTHDAY TO YOU —

'Happy Birthday To You' was written in the 1890s by schoolteacher Mildred Hill. The lyrics were thought up by Mildred's sister Patti, also a teacher, and were originally 'Good morning to all'. The song became increasingly popular in schools across the USA and Patti eventually changed the lyrics to 'Happy birthday to you'. This altered version was published in 1935 and popularised in the Broadway production of *A Thousand Cheers*. In 1988, Birch Tree Group Ltd sold the rights of the song to Warner Communications for a cool $28 million (£19 million). Along with 'Auld Lang Syne' and 'For He's A Jolly Good Fellow', the song is one of the three most popular songs in the English language. It was also the first song to be sung in outer space, by the Apollo IX astronauts on 8 March 1969.

— EDITH PIAF'S FUNERAL —

...was the only occasion after World War II that Parisian traffic came to a complete standstill. There were so many people at the event that allegedly several mourners fell into the open grave.

— THE SEVEN MOVEMENTS OF DANCE —

Jean-Georges Noverre (1727–1810) was a dancer, a choreographer and a teacher of dancers. He also wrote *Lettres sur la Danse et sur les Ballets* ('Letters on Dance and Ballet', 1761), the most important book on ballet published in the 18th century and possibly one of the most important dance manuals of all time. He is credited with defining the seven movements of dance thus:

Bend • Glide • Turn • Stretch • Jump • Rise • Dart

— NOTABLE SCAT SINGERS —

Louis Armstrong
Cab Calloway
Ella Fitzgerald
Slim Gaillard
Benny Carter
Dizzy Gillespie
Anita O'Day
Scatman Crothers
The Nutty Squirrels
Louis Prima

— CHILLA —

The Chilla ritual is a highly mysterious and spiritual phenomenon which Indian musicians are required to undertake three times in their lives. The procedure lasts for 40 days and usually takes place in a hut in a remote region near the village of the musician's guru's ancestors. The musician plays intensely all day, every day, and reports of hallucinations and visions are not uncommon. The ultimate aim of the ritual is for the musician to conquer their demons and defeat their artistic insecurities, leaving him/her to explore musical and creative possibilities they would otherwise perhaps never have encountered.

MAKIN' BABIES MIXTAPE — (MUSIC TO MAKE LOVE TO) —

'Let's Get It On' – Marvin Gaye
'Je T'aime (Moi Non Plus)' – Serge Gainsbourg with Jane Birkin
'Mystic Lady' – T Rex
'I Put A Spell On You' – Screamin' Jay Hawkins
'Sexual Healing' – Marvin Gaye
'Let's Stay Together' – Al Green
'Lady' – D'Angelo
'If I Was Your Girlfriend' – Prince
'Lovin' You' – Minnie Riperton
'I'm Gonna Love You' – Barry White
'Rock Me Tonight (For Old Times' Sake)' – Freddie Jackson
'Cupid' – Sam Cooke
'One Love' – Massive Attack
'Come With Me' – Teddy Pendergrass
'Sign Your Name' – Terence Trent D'Arby
'The Sweetest Taboo' – Sade
'Baby, What You Want Me To Do' – Etta James
'You're Making Me High' – Toni Braxton
'(You Make Me Feel Like) A Natural Woman' – Aretha Franklin

THE WORLD'S MOST — VALUABLE JAZZ INSTRUMENT —

A saxophone once owned by Charlie Parker was sold for £93,500 ($144,500) at Christie's in South Kensington, London, on 7 September 1994.

— TAKE ME OUT TO THE BALL-GAME —

The song sung at every seventh inning at every baseball game at every park in the USA was written by Jack Norworth on some scrap paper during a train ride to Manhattan, New York, in 1908. Norworth gave the lyrics to his friend Albert Von Tilzer, who composed the music. The song became a hit, despite the fact that neither Norworth or Von Tilzer had been to a baseball game when the song was published.

Nelly Kelly loved baseball games,
Knew the players, knew all their names,
You could see her there ev'ry day,
Shout 'Hurray' when they'd play.
Her boyfriend by the name of Joe
Said, 'To Coney Isle, dear, let's go',
Then Nelly started to fret and pout,
And to him I heard her shout:
'Take me out to the ball game,
Take me out with the crowd.
Buy me some peanuts and Crackerjack,
I don't care if I never get back,
Let me root, root, root for the home team,
If they don't win, it's a shame.
For it's one, two, three strikes, you're out,
At the old ball game.'

Nelly Kelly was sure some fan,
She would root just like any man,
Told the umpire he was wrong,
All along, good and strong.
When the score was just two to two,
Nelly Kelly knew what to do,
Just to cheer up the boys she knew,
She made the game sing this song.
'Take me out to the ball game,
Take me out with the crowd.
Buy me some peanuts and Crackerjack,
I don't care if I never get back,
Let me root, root, root for the home team,
If they don't win, it's a shame.
For it's one, two, three strikes, you're out,
At the old ball game.'

— PAYOLA —

'Payola' is a composite of the words *pay* and *Victrola* (a brand of LP record player). It entered the English language via the record business following the infamous 'payola scandal' of the '60s and has come to mean the paying of cash or gifts in exchange for airplay. The first court case involving payola took place in 1960, and resulted in radio DJ and personality Alan Freed being indicted for accepting $2,500 (£1,750), which he claimed was a token of gratitude and did not affect airplay. After paying a small fine, he was released, but his career took a downhill turn and in 1965 he drank himself to death. After the trial, the anti-payola statute was passed, under which payola became illegal with a penalty of up to $10,000 (£6,500) in fines and one year in prison.

— THE SELF-LOVE MIX TAPE — (MUSIC TO LOVE YOURSELF TO)

Tubeway Army – 'Every Day I Die'
The Buzzcocks – 'Orgasm Addict'
Tism – 'Been Caught Wankin''
New Order – 'The Perfect Kiss'
The Fauves – 'Self Abuser'
Elvis Costello – 'Pump It Up'
Frenzal Rhomb – 'Be Still My Beating Off'
Billy Squier – 'The Stroke'
The Boys Next Door – 'Masturbation Generation'
The Vapours – 'Turning Japanese'
Frank Zappa – 'Ms Pinky'
The Violent Femmes – 'Blister In The Sun'
The Who – 'Pictures Of Lily'
Radiohead – 'Thinking About You'
Faith No More – 'Jizzlobber'
Billy Idol – 'Dancing With Myself'
The Divinyls – 'I Touch Myself'
Iggy Pop – 'I'm Bored'
The Cure – 'Close To Me'
Chuck Berry – 'My Ding-A-Ling'

— FAMOUS 52ND STREET JAZZ CLUBS (NYC) —

The Spotlite
The Yacht Club
The Three Deuces
Jimmy Ryan's
Onyx
The Royal Roost*
The Famous Door
Downbeat
Kelly's Stables*
Hickory House*
Tondelayo's

**Denotes venues a block or more away from 52nd Street.*

— SHOW ME HOW TO DO THE HULA (LYRICS) —

Lyrics and music: Mel Peterson

Show me how to do the Hula,
Like they do in Honolulu,
When they dance the Hula-Hula,
To Honi Ka Ua Wiki-Wiki.
First you sway and move your hands,
Like the waves fall on the sands,
And then you smile a pretty smile,
To Honi Ka Ua Wiki-Wiki.
Around the island you must go,
You move so sweet and slow,
And then you sway just like the trees,
As they're caught in a tropic breeze.
Now you've learned to do the Hula,
Like they do in Honolulu,
Where they dance the Hula-Hula,
To Honi Ka Ua Wiki-Wiki.

— SALSA —

Salsa literally means 'sauce'. The phrase came into use in the '60s to describe a range of Latin and Afro-Latin music from Cuban son montuno, bebop, Cubop, Puerto Rican bomba, plena, Dominican merengue, Afro-American jazz and rhythm and blues.

— SPEED YODELLING —

The fastest yodel was 22 tones (15 falsetto) in one second on 9 February 1992, performed by Thomas Scholl of Munich, Germany.

THE EIGHT SEAS THROUGH WHICH THE — BEATLES' YELLOW SUBMARINE TRAVELS —

Time
Music
Science
Monsters
Consumer Products
Nowhere
Green Phrenology
Holes

— TROPICALISTAS —

The word Tropicália came originally from a 1967 ambient-art piece by Brazilian artist Hélio Oiticica, but it was adopted by a group of Brazilian musicians who sought to redefine Brazilian culture. A short-lived but explosive late-'60s/early-'70s movement, Tropicalia musicians actively attempted to subvert the military dictatorship that had taken over the country in 1964 and many were subsequently exiled or imprisoned. The artists combined rock, blues, jazz, folk and psychedelic music with Brazilian and other Latin-American styles and created an exciting and revolutionary environment that questioned the long-standing dominance of bossa nova. Tropicalia musicians included:

Gilberto Gil
Tom Ze
Caetano Veloso
Maria Bethania
Jorge Ben
Gal Costa
Os Mutantes

— THE DOPPLER EFFECT —

Named after the Austrian scientist Christian Doppler (1803–1853), the Doppler effect refers to the apparent change in the frequency of a wave (ie sound or light) when the source of the wave and the observer are in motion relative to one another. The frequency of the wave increases when the source and observer are approaching each other and decreases when they are moving away from each other, creating the impression of a change in pitch (ie a police car siren apparently sounding at a higher pitch the closer it gets).

— HOW TO PLAY THE SPOONS (STEP BY STEP) —

- Place one spoon between your pointer finger and middle finger.
- Wrap your middle finger around back of the spoon and press the edge against your palm.
- Rest the handle of the spoon on the central joint of the middle finger.
- Place the other spoon between thumb and first finger, laying it across the middle bone of your index finger.
- Wrap your index finger around the back of the spoon and hold it tightly against the palm, pressing down with the thumb to achieve good purchase.
- Ensure that the bottoms of the spoon bowls are back to back, allowing for half an inch of space.
- Put your hand, palm down, about seven inches above your leg.
- Start by hitting the spoons down on your leg and up on your palm.

— STARS AND STRIPES FOREVER —

* John Philip Sousa's 'Star And Stripes Forever' is never played at the circus unless there is some sort of emergency, when it is then used as a secret warning signal.

Let martial note in triumph float,
And liberty extend its mighty hand.
A flag appears 'mid thunderous cheers,
The banner of the Western land.
The emblem of the brave and true,
Its folds protect no tyrant crew;
The red and white and starry blue
Is freedom's shield and hope.
Other nations may deem their flags the best
And cheer them with fervid elation,
But the flag of the North and South and West
Is the flag of flags, the flag of Freedom's nation.
Hurrah for the flag of the free!
May it wave as our standard forever,
The gem of the land and the sea,
The banner of the right.
Let despots remember the day
When our fathers with mighty endeavor
Proclaimed as they marched to the fray,
That by their might and by their right
It waves forever.
Let eagle shriek from lofty peak
The never-ending watchword of our land;
Let summer breeze waft through the trees
The echo of the chorus grand.
Sing out for liberty and light,
Sing out for freedom and the right.
Sing out for Union and its might,
O patriotic sons.
Other nations may deem their flags the best
And cheer them with fervid elation,
But the flag of the North and South and West
Is the flag of flags, the flag of Freedom's nation.
Hurrah for the flag of the free.
May it wave as our standard forever
The gem of the land and the sea,
The banner of the right.
Let despots remember the day
When our fathers with might endeavor
Proclaimed as they marched to the fray,
That by their might and by their right
It waves forever.

— SOME ROLLING STONES TRIBUTE BANDS —

The Railing Stains • Rolling Clones • Strolling Bones • Stolling Rones • The Rollin' Stoned • Rolling Stones Story • Le Pietre Rotolanti (Italian)

— THOMAS EDISON'S TEN SUGGESTED USES — FOR HIS PHONOGRAPH INVENTION

Thomas Alva Edison (1847–1931) invented the phonograph in 1877. Famously, he was not initially interested in using the machine for entertainment purposes. The following are the ten different uses he proposed that his new invention could be put to:

1) Letter writing and all kinds of dictation without the aid of a stenographer.
2) Phonographic books, which will speak to blind people without effort on their part.
3) The teaching of elocution.
4) The reproduction of music.
5) The 'family record' – a registry of sayings, reminiscences, etc, by members of a family in their own voices, and of the last words of dying persons.
6) Music boxes and toys.
7) Clocks that should announce in articulate speech the time for going home, going to meals, etc.
8) The preservation of languages by exact reproduction of the manner of pronouncing.
9) Educational purposes, such as preserving the explanations made by a teacher, so that the pupil can refer to them at any moment, and spelling or other lessons placed upon the phonograph for convenience in committing to memory.
10) Connection with the telephone, so as to make that instrument an auxiliary in the transmission of permanent and invaluable records, instead of being the recipient of momentary and fleeting communication.

— STYLE DYNAMICS —

Amoroso	Tender and affectionate
Animato	Animated; lively
Calando	Gradually softer and slower
Cantabile	In a singing style
Con anima	With life and animation
Con brio	With vigour and spirit
Con fuoco	With energy or passion
Deciso	Decisively
Detache	Detached
Dolce	Sweetly
Doloroso	Sorrowfully
Espressivo	Expressively
Furioso	Furiously
Giocoso	Humorously
Grandioso	With grandeur
Grazioso	Gracefully
Legato	Smooth and connected
Leggiero	Lightly
Maestoso	Majestically
Marcato	Marked and stressed
Marzial	In the style of a march
Morendo	Dying away
Perdendosi	Dying away
Pesante	Heavy
Religioso	Religiously, solemnly
Rubato	Taken out of tempo
Semplice	Simple
Sempre	Always, continuously
Sostenuto	Sustained
Soto voce	In an undertone
Staccato	Short and detached

— THE RAREST RECORD IN THE WORLD —

The rarest record in the world is the original *The Freewheelin' Bob Dylan* LP. There are many different existing versions of this album, but the most sought after is a mint copy of the stereo album that has the original tracks listed on the sleeve, the labels and the record. These copies are worth approximately \$25,000–\$30,000 (£17,000–£22,000).

— TOP-SELLING SINGLES OF ALL TIME —

1 'Candle In The Wind', Elton John (1997) – 37 million+

2 'White Christmas', Bing Crosby (1943) – 30 million+

3 'Rock Around The Clock', Bill Haley And The Comets (1954) – 17 million+

4 'I Want To Hold Your Hand', The Beatles (1963) – 12 million+

5 'Hey Jude', The Beatles (1968) – 10 million+

5 'It's Now Or Never', Elvis Presley (1960) – 10 million+

5 'I Will Always Love You', Whitney Houston (1993) – 10 million+

8 'Hound Dog'/'Don't Be Cruel', Elvis Presley (1956) – 9 million+

8 'Diana', Paul Anka (1957) – 9 million+

10 'I'm A Believer', The Monkees (1966) – 8 million+

10 '(Everything I Do) I Do It For You', Bryan Adams (1991) – 8 million+

— THE FIRST VIENNA VEGETABLE ORCHESTRA —

The instruments in the First Vienna Vegetable Orchestra are made, unsurprisingly, from vegetables, although additional kitchen utensils, such as knives and mixers, are sometimes played. The vegetables are amplified by a combination of microphones The musical repertoire of the orchestra is impressively broad, ranging from traditional African pieces to classical European concert music through to experimental electronic sounds. The orchestra consists of eight musicians, a sound technician and a chef, who blends the instruments into a soup after each performance and shares it amongst the players and the audience. The orchestra are at pains to point out that they are not all vegetarian.

— PIANO FACTS —

The piano was invented by Bartolommeo Cristofori in Italy in 1709.

Interesting early designs included the giraffe piano, in which the wing-shaped body extended towards the ceiling. There was also a piano with six keyboards.

On early fortepianos, the 'pedal' was often manipulated by the knees.

The first piano built in America was made by John Brent of Philadelphia in 1774.

The lowest note on the piano sounds at 27.500Hz.

The highest note is the top C, which sounds at 4186.009Hz.

The ideal humidity for a piano is 40–50%.

The average piano has 88 keys. Of these, 36 are black keys, commonly known as 'sharps' and 'flats', depending on the key in which they are played.

The piano is not capable of playing the full 'chromatic' scale.

Although the average piano has around 230 strings, it is considered to be a percussion instrument by symphony orchestras because its strings are struck.

— CYNTHIA 'PLASTER CASTER' ALBRITTON —

Over the last 30 years, Cynthia Albritton has been making plaster casts from the genitals of musicians. After two years of experimenting with Jimi Hendrix, she finally perfected her method and has since moulded the following artists, amongst others...

Jimi Hendrix (guitarist)
Noel Redding (bass player, The Jimi Hendrix Experience)
Bob Pridden (road manager, The Who)
Richard Cole (tour manager, Led Zeppelin)
Dennis Thompson (drummer, The MC5)
Wayne Kramer (guitarist, The MC5)

— CYNTHIA 'PLASTER CASTER' ALBRITTON (CONT'D) —

Fritz Richmond (jug bass player, The Jim Kweskin Jug Band)
Anthony Newley (singer/songwriter)
Eddie Brigati (singer, The Young Rascals)
Lee Mallory (singer/songwriter)
John Barr (bass player, The Churls)
Bob Henrit (drummer, Argent, The Kinks)
Zal Yanovsky (The Lovin' Spoonful)
Ricky Fataar (drummer, The Beach Boys, Bonnie Raitt, The Rutles)
John Smothers (bodyguard, Frank Zappa)
Jon Langford (singer/guitarist, The Mekons, The Three Johns)
Chris Connelley (singer, Revolting Cocks)
Clint Poppie (singer, Pop Will Eat Itself)
Jello Biafra (singer, The Dead Kennedys)
Richard Lloyd (guitarist, Television, Matthew Sweet)
Eric Burdon (singer, The Animals)*
Suzi Gardner (lead guitarist and singer, L7)*
Christine Doll Rod (drummer, Demolition Doll Rods)*
Laetitia Sadier (singer/keyboards, Stereolab)*
Peaches (singer/songwriter)*
Sally Timms (singer, The Mekons)*

**In the case of girls, breasts were cast..*

— 'MADCHESTER' BANDS —

In 1989, the English city of Manchester became the coolest musical place on Earth as bands combined sleazy guitar rock with the emerging ecstasy/acid-house ethic. Here are some of the bands who caught the Madchester wave:

The Happy Mondays
The Charlatans
The Stone Roses
The Inspiral Carpets
The Joy Division
The Mock Turtles
Northside
New Order
Sub Sub
New Fast Automatic Daffodils
MC Tunes
The High
808 State
A Guy Called Gerald

— PAGE OF CAGE —

John Cage is a colossus of 20th Century music. Throughout his long and distinguished career, he has worked primarily within the avant garde, experimenting with everything from prepared pianos to odd percussion instruments and rhythmic arrangements, silence, and strange notational systems. The principal protagonist of indeterminism, Cage often incorporated Zen philosophy into his music. His influence on younger generations of musicians, composers and artists of all kinds has been profound.

'The idea of a mistake is beside the point, for once anything happens, it authentically is.'

'I have nothing to say. And I am saying it. And that is poetry. As I needed it.'

'If something is boring after two minutes, try it for four. If still boring, then eight. Then 16. Then 32. Eventually one discovers that it is not boring at all.'

'The first question I ask myself when something doesn't seem to be beautiful is why do I think it's not beautiful. And very shortly you discover that there is no reason.'

'As far as consistency of thought goes, I prefer inconsistency.'

If someone says can't, that shows you what to do.'

'There is poetry as soon as we realise that we possess nothing.'

'I can't understand why people are frightened of new ideas. I'm frightened of the old ones.'

'We need not destroy the past. It is gone.'

'There is no such thing as an empty space or an empty time. There is always something to see, something to hear. In fact, try as we may to make a silence, we cannot.'

— TIN PAN ALLEY —

Tin Pan Alley was a nickname given to Manhattan's West 28th Street (between Broadway and Sixth Avenue), where many of the fledgling publishers of popular music had their offices. In time, it became the generic term for all publishers of popular American sheet music, regardless of their geographic locations. Legend has is that the nickname came about after a *New York Tribune* reporter wrote a story on a composer called Von Tilzer, who put newspapers behind piano strings in order to get an odd, high-pitched sound when he played. Upon arriving at the building, the reporter heard a 'tinny' sound created by the tinkling of these pianos. When the article was published, it described Von Tilzer as 'Mr Tin Pan Alley...'

THE SUICIDE MIX TAPE — (MUSIC TO KILL YOURSELF TO) —

'Won't You Come To My Funeral?' – Garbo
'Hurt' – Nine Inch Nails
'Goodbye' Prince
'Everybody Hurts' – REM
'Fade To Black' – Metallica
'Wave Of Mutilation' – The Pixies
'Bohemian Rhapsody' – Queen
'Killing Me Softly With His Song' – Roberta Flack
'Rape Me' – Nirvana
'Goodbye Cruel World' – Pink Floyd
'Die Young' – Black Sabbath
'Crucify' – Tori Amos
'Suicide Is Painless' (M*A*S*H Theme) – M Altman and J Mandel
'Suffer' – Smashing Pumpkins
'Stan' – Eminem
'Suicide Solution' – Ozzy Osbourne
'How Long Will They Mourn Me?' – Tupac Shakur
'Last Resort' – Papa Roach

— ON CRITICS —

'If a literary man puts together two words about music, one of them will be wrong.' *Aaron Copland*

'Can't you listen to chords without knowing their names?' *Claude Debussy*

'A musicologist is a man who can read music but can't hear it.' *Sir Thomas Beecham*

'The lot of critics is to be remembered by what they failed to understand.' *George Moore*

'Critics love mediocrity.' *Giacomo Puccini*

'Dear sir and friend, not only are you an arse, but you are an unmusical arse...' *Erik Satie to the critic Jean Poueigh*

'Last year I gave several lectures on intelligence and musicality in animals. I shall speak to you today about intelligence and musicality in critics. The subject is very similar...' *Erik Satie*

'The immoral profession of music criticism must be abolished.' *Richard Wagner*

'Pay no attention to what the critics say; no statue has ever been put up to a critic.' *Jean Sibelius*

'I have just read your review of Margaret's concert... Someday I hope to meet you. When that happens, you'll need a new nose, a lot of beefsteak for black eyes and perhaps a supporter below.' *Harry S Truman in a letter to Paul Hume, music critic of the* Washington Post, *after an unkind review of Truman's daughter's vocal prowess*

'If the music doesn't say it, how many words can say it for the music?' *John Coltrane*

'Writing about music is like dancing about architecture' *Attributed to various*

'Most rock journalism is people who can't write interviewing people who can't talk for people who can't read.' *Frank Zappa*

'Asking a musician what he thinks about critics is like asking a lamppost how it feels about dogs.' *Anonymous*

— TIMELINE OF SELECTED CLASSICAL COMPOSERS —

1369–1453: John Dunstable
1399–1474: Guillaume Dufay
1450–1517: Heinrich Isaak
1505–1585: Thomas Tallis
1532–1594: Orlando Di Lasso
1567–1643: Claudio Monteverdi
1675–1741: Antonio Vivaldi
1685–1757: Domenico Scarlatti
1585–1672: Heinrich Schutz
1685–1750: Johann Sebastian Bach
1685–1759: George Friederich Händel
1562–1628: John Bull
1659–1695: Henry Purcell
1632–1687: Jean-Baptiste Lully
1681–1767: Georg Philipp Telemann
1714–1788: Carl Philipp Emanuel Bach
1732–1809: Franz Joseph Haydn
1756–1791: Wolfgang Amadeus Mozart
1770–1827: Ludwig Van Beethoven
1786–1826: Carl Maria Von Weber
1797–1847: Gaetano Donizetti
1801–1835: Vincenzo Bellini
1797–1828: Franz Schubert
1803–1869: Hector Berlioz
1809–1847: Felix Mendelssohn
1810–1849: Frederic Chopin
1810–1856: Robert Schumann
1811–1886: Franz Liszt
1819–1896: Clara Wiek-Schumann
1813–1901: Guiseppe Verdi
1813–1883: Richard Wagner
1825–1899: Johann Strauss
1833–1897: Johannes Brahms
1834–1887: Aleksandr Porfyrevich Borodin
1838–1875: Georges Bizet
1840–1893: Peter Illich Tchaikovsky
1841–1904: Anton Dvořák
1842–1900: Sir Arthur Sullivan
1844–1908: Nikolai Andreyevich Rimsky-Korsakov
1858–1924: Giacomo Puccini

1860–1911: Gustav Mahler
1862–1918: Claude Debussy
1873–1943: Sergei Rachmaninoff
1872–1915: Alexander Scriabin
1874–1951: Arnold Schoenberg
1875–1937: Maurice Ravel
1881–1945: Bela Bartók
1882–1971: Igor Stravinsky
1883–1945: Anton Von Webern
1885–1935: Alban Berg
1891–1953: Sergei Prokofiev
1895–1963: Paul Hindemith
1899–1963: Francis Poulenc
1900–1950: Kurt Weill
1900–1990: Aaron Copland
1902–1983: William Walton
1906–1975: Dmitri Shostakovich
1908–1992: Olivier Messiaen
1913–1976: Benjamin Britten

— NATIONAL ANTHEMS: THE LONG AND THE SHORT —

The Greek national anthem, 'Innos Pros Tin Eleftherian' ('The Hymn To Liberty'), is officially the longest national anthem in the world, with 158 verses. Two African countries – Qatar and Bahrain – can lay claim to having the shortest national anthems, since neither of theirs have any words. The shortest national anthem with lyrics is the Japanese, which is four lines long – the lyrics consist of 32 syllables, written 1,000 years ago, and celebrate longevity of seniors.

— KARAOKE —

A Japanese abbreviated compound word: 'kara' comes from 'karappo' meaning 'empty', and 'oke' is the abbreviation of 'okesutura' or 'orchestra'. Thus 'kara-oke' literally means 'empty orchestra'.

— RAPRONYMS AND HIP-HOP INITIALS —

Big Daddy Kane – *King Asiatic Nobody's Equal*
B.O.X. – *Beyond Ordinary X-Istence*
Dl – *Down Low*
Dmx – *Dark Man Of The Unknown*
KRS One – *Knowledge Rules Supreme Over Nearly Everybody*
Kool G Rap – *Kool Genius Of Rap*
Guru – *Gifted Unlimited Rhymes Universal*
LL Cool J – *Ladies Love Col James*
Ja Rule – *Jeff Atkins Represents Unconditional Love's Existence*
The Beastie Boys – *Boys Entering Anarchistic States Towards Internal Excellence*
Black Moon – *Brothers Lyrically Acting Combining Kicking Music Out On Nations*
ED OG And Da Bulldogs – *EveryDay Other Girls And Da Black United Leaders Living Directly Off Grooving Sounds*
MOP– *Mash-Out Posse*
Goodie Mob – *The Good Die Mostly Over Bullshit*
Junior Mafia – *Masters At Finding Intelligent Attitudes*
KMD – *Kausin' Much Damage, or A Positive Kause In A Much-Damaged Society*
The Lox – *Livin' Off X-Perience*
Wu-Tang Clan – *We Usually Take All Niggas Garments; Witty Unpredictable Talent And Natural Game*
Yaggfu Front – *You Are Gonna Get Fucked Up If You Front*
Tash – *Tough As Son Of Harold*

— THE FOUR MAIN PRINCIPLES OF THE MIGHTY FIVE —

In the late 19th century, the Russian composers Modest Mussorgsky (1839–1881), Mily Balakirev (1837–1910), Alexander Borodin (1833–1887), Cesar Cui (1835–1918) and Nikolay Rimsky-Korsakov (1844–1908) joined together to form a group known as 'The Mighty Five' (aka 'The Mighty Handful'). Feeling disillusioned with the academic musical establishment, they sought a fresh approach to composition. Using folk song, modal and exotic scales, and folk polyphony, they re-introduced Russian folk music into the classical genre. Their four main principles were:

To use Russian themes and history as subjects for music.

To adapt western European styles to fit that of Russia's folk harmonies and musicality.

To advocate realism.

To favour the spirit and style of 19th-century Romanticism and reject Classicism.

— TONE CLUSTERS —

Tone clusters are harmonies based on diatonic seconds rather than thirds in piano-music notation – that is, they are more tightly grouped than normal chords. The effect of these clusters is one of stirring dissonance, and they are usually produced on the piano by depressing a segment of the keyboard with a fist, a forearm, or a board of specified length. They were introduced by Henry Cowell (1897–1965), a controversial composer who also utilised direct manipulation of the piano strings with his hands, plucking them as he played. In 1920 Cowell was dubbed 'the loudest pianist in the world'.

— PATRONS OF THE LIVERPOOL INSTITUTE FOR — PERFORMING ARTS (LIPA)

Joan Armatrading, Dame Jocelyn Barrow, David Bedford, Sir Richard Branson, Graham Collier, John Dankworth, Dame Judi Dench, John Gunter, Glyn Johns, Mark Knopfler, Gillian Lynne, Sir Cameron Mackintosh, Sir George Martin, Robert North, Lady Olivier, Sir Alan Parker, Monica Parker, Lord David Puttnam, Lou Reed, Paul Scofield, Alpana Sengupta, Carly Simon, Peter Sissons, Wayne Sleep, Toyah Willcox, Victoria Wood, Jon Vangelis.

* The LIPA was founded by Sir Paul McCartney in 1996.

— ENTRAINMENT —

The discovery of entrainment is connected to Dutch scientist Christian Huygens (1629–1695), who, while working on the design of the pendulum clock, found that, when he placed two pendulums on a wall near each other and swung them at different rates, they eventually ended up synchronising with each other. This mutual influence is called *entrainment* and applies to many fields of science and physics including chemistry, pharmacology, biology, medicine, psychology, sociology, astronomy, architecture and others. In resonance entrainment, for example, if a tuning fork designed to produce a frequency of 440Hz is vibrating close to another 440Hz tuning fork, the second fork will also begin to oscillate without being physically touched. Entrainment is used as a tool in music therapy, encouraging the brain to relax with slow, soothing music.

— CLASSICAL MUSIC ERAS —

Dark Ages (AD 475–1000)
High Middle Ages (1000–1350)
Late Middle Ages (1350–1500)
Early Renaissance (1400–1517)
Late Renaissance (1517–1600)
Italian Baroque (1600–1750)
German/English/French Baroque (1650–1750)
Rococo (1700–1750)
Classical (1750–1820)
Early Romantic (1790–1820)
Late Romantic (1850–1900)
Modern (1900–1945)
Contemporary (present day)

— MARIE TAGLIONI —

In 1842 Marie Taglioni (1804–1884), a ballerina famous for dancing *Le Sylphides*, put glue and horse hair on her ballet slippers to make them stiff enough to stand on the tips of her toes. Although she wasn't the first person to dance on her toes (also known as *pointe*), her inimitable grace and fluidity popularised the technique. When Taglioni made her final guest appearance in Russia in 1842, a group of St Petersburg groupies allegedly paid 200 roubles for a pair of her old shoes – then cooked them and ate them with a special sauce.

— THE TANGO —

The origins of the tango lie in the late 19th century in Argentinian bars, gambling houses, and brothels. The dance was originally conceived as an acting-out of the relationship between a prostitute and her pimp. As such, many of the early tangos had distinctly sexual undertones. Because the male-female dance was regarded as obscene, men found it difficult to find female partners outside the brothels and turned to each other as partners. Enactments of man-on-man combat (duelling) to win the favours of a woman became common, which explains why the tango is sometimes referred to as 'a dance between two men'.

— HARPSICHORD FRENCH-ENGLISH LEXICON —

Balance Pin Pointe de Balancement
Belly Rail Contre-Sommier
Bentside Eclisse Courbe
Choir Choeur
Damper Etouffoir
Double Harpsichord Clavecin à Deux Claviers
Harpsichord Clavecin
Hitchpin Pointe D'accroche
Key Touche
Keyboard Clavier
Pitch Hauteur, Diapason
Plectrum Plectre, Bec
Rank Rang
Stop Jeu
Stop Lever Lévier de Régistration, Tirette
Tail Queue
Tongue Languette
Transposing Transpositeur
Tuning Fork Diapason
Voicing Harmonisation
Wrest Pin Cheville D'accord

— INTRIGUING INSPIRATIONS —

Artist	Song	Year
Paul Simon	'Mother And Child Reunion'	1972
Inspiration: A chicken-and-egg dish on a Chinese restaurant menu		
Otis Blackwell	'All Shook Up'	1957
Inspiration: A bottle of Pepsi		
Willie Nelson	'Who'll Buy My Memories'	1991
Inspiration: The loss of $16 million (£10 million) in back taxes to the IRS		
Tommy James And The Shondells	'Mony Mony'	1968
Inspiration: The neon sign of the Mutual Of New York insurance building		
Thomas Durden And Mae Boren Axton	'Heartbreak Hotel'	1956
Inspiration: A newspaper story relating a suicide note		
Phil Spector	'To Know Him Is To Love Him'	1958
Inspiration: Words on his father's tombstone		
Jackson Browne	'Running On Empty'	1977
Inspiration: An empty petrol tank		
Otis Redding	'Respect'	1965
Inspiration: A conversation between Otis and Al Jackson		
Holland, Dozier, Holland	'Stop In The Name Of Love'	1965
Inspiration: A comment made by Dozier during a fight with his girlfriend		
Sam And Dave	'Hold On, I'm Coming'	1966
Inspiration: David Porter's response to Isaac Hayes' when Hayes told him to hurry up out of the toilet.		

— JOHN BUBBLES —

John Bubbles (born John Sublett in Louisville, Kentucky, in 1902) was the tap dancer who introduced the technique of dropping the heel to add more rhythmic flexibility. The technique, known as the 'rhythm tap', uses the toe as the treble and the heel as the bass, allowing for a broader combination of steps and sounds. Before Bubbles, dancers tended to dance flat-footed or on their toes. Along with Bill 'Bojangles' Robinson (who started the form of tapping on one's toes), John Bubbles is often cited as one of the two most influential artists in tap dancing.

— BRITISH VS AMERICAN TERMS FOR MUSICAL NOTES —

US	UK
Whole Note	Semibreve
Half Note	Minim
Quarter Note	Crotchet
Eighth Note	Quaver
16th Note	Semiquaver
32nd Note	Demi-semiquaver
64th Note	Hemi-demi-semiquaver
128th Note	Quasi-hemi-demi-semiquaver

— MAIN TYPES OF MICROPHONE —

Dynamic Microphones
Condenser Microphones
Large-Diaphragm Condenser Microphones
Electret Microphones
Plaintalk Microphones
Ribbon Microphones
Carbon-Granule Microphones

**Speciality Microphones:*
Wireless, Lavalier, Bass, Pressure-Zone

— UNDERSTANDING OPERA –

Opera: The plural of the Latin word *opus*, meaning 'work'. The word is a shortened form of the Italian *opera in musica*, or 'works in music'.

PERSONS DEPICTED ON THE COVER OF — *SERGEANT PEPPER'S LONELY HEARTS CLUB BAND* —

The classic cover of *Sergeant Pepper's* was designed by Peter Blake, and the photos were taken by Michael Cooper at Chelsea Manor Photographic Studios on 30 March 1967. The set featured life-sized cardboard cut-outs of all the figures – musical, cultural and political – who influenced The Beatles. Several people who were intended to be included on the cover never made it, including Elvis, Hitler and Jesus. Also, two people who were included were later removed by photographic retouching. Leo Gorcey was removed because he requested a fee, and Ghandi, because EMI felt his inclusion might offend record buyers in India.

1. Sri Yukteswar Giri
2. Aleister Crowley
3. Mae West
4. Lenny Bruce
5. Karlheinz Stockhausen
6. WC (William Claude) Fields
7. Carl Gustav Jung
8. Edgar Allan Poe
9. Fred Astaire
10. Richard Merkin

11. The Varga Girl
12. Leo Gorcey
13. Huntz Hall
14. Simon Rodia
15. Bob Dylan
16. Aubrey Beardsley
17. Sir Robert Peel
18. Aldous Huxley
19. Dylan Thomas
20. Terry Southern
21. Dion (Di Mucci)
22. Tony Curtis
23. Wallace Berman
24. Tommy Handley
25. Marylin Monroe
26. William Burroughs
27. Sri Mahavatara Babji
28. Stan Laurel
29. Richard Lindner
30. Oliver Hardy
31. Karl Marx
32. HG (Herbert George) Wells
33. Sri Paramahansa Yogananda
34. Anonymous
35. Stuart Sutcliffe
36. Anonymous
37. Max Miller
38. The Petty Girl
39. Marlon Brando
40. Tom Mix
41. Oscar Wilde
42. Tyrone Power
43. Larry Bell
44. Dr David Livingstone
45. Johnny Weismuller
46. Stephen Crane
47. Issy Bonn
48. George Bernard Shaw
49. HC (Horace Clifford) Westermann
50. Albert Stubbins
51. Sri Lahiri Mahasaya
52. Lewis Carroll
53. TE (Thomas Edward) Lawrence (Of Arabia)
54. Sonny Listen
55. The Petty Girl
56. George Harrison
57. John Lennon
58. Shirley Temple
59. Ringo Starr
60. Paul McCartney
61. Albert Einstein
62. John Lennon
63. Ringo Starr
64. Paul McCartney
65. George Harrison
66. Bobby Breen
67. Marlene Dietrich
68. Mohandas Karamchand Ghandi
69. Legionnaire From The Order Of The Buffalos
70. Diana Dors
71. Shirley Temple
72. Cloth Grandmother-Figure
73. Shirley Temple
74. Mexican Candlestick
75. Television Set
76. Stone Figure Of Girl
77. Stone Figure
78. Statue From John Lennon's House
79. Trophy
80. Four-Armed Indian Doll
81. Drum Skin
82. Hookah
83. Velvet Snake
84. Japanese Stone Figure
85. Snow White
86. Garden Gnome
87. Tuba

THE FIRST WOMAN TO CONDUCT — THE METROPOLITAN OPERA (NEW YORK CITY) —

Sarah Caldwell, an American opera director and conductor, founded the Opera Company of Boston in 1957 and served as its artistic director and frequently as its conductor. She became the first woman to conduct at the Met in 1976.

— LIMITED BUT POTENTIALLY USEFUL — GLOSSARY OF OPERA TERMS

- **Aria (Italian)** – extended musical piece performed by one singer.
- **Bel canto** – Italian for 'beautiful singing', where the beauty of the singing is more important than the plot or the words.
- **Cadenza (Italian)** – a brilliant passage inserted in an aria which gives the singer an opportunity to show off their voice.
- **Commedia dell'arte (Italian)** – popular style of opera in Italy from the 16th century onwards; plots frequently revolved around disguises, mistaken identities and misunderstandings.
- **Crescendo (Italian)** — a gradual increase in volume.
- **Diva (Italian)** – an important female opera star.
- **Finale ultimo (Italian)** – the final finale.
- **Imbroglio (Italian)** – operatic scene in which diversity of rhythm and melody create chaos and confusion.
- **Intermezzo (Italian)** – short musical passage between acts.
- **Libretto (Italian)** – Italian for 'little book' – the text of an opera.
- **Prima Donna (Italian)** — the leading woman singer in an opera.
- **Ritornello (Italian)** – instrumental prelude to an individual song within a cantata, concerto or aria
- **Roulade (French), or run** – quick succession of notes sung to one syllable.
- **Soubrette (French)** – female character with a light soprano voice.
- **Supernumerary** – performer who doesn't sing.
- **Trouser role** – a role which depicts a young man or boy but is sung by a woman.

— SYMPHONY I: THE GOTHIC (1919-1927) —

One of the biggest symphonies ever created, *The Gothic*, was composed by Havergal Brian (1876–1972). The performance calls for more than 1,000 musicians forming an enormous orchestra of strings comprising 32 woodwinds, 24 brass instruments, two timpanists (supplemented by 17 additional percussionists), two harps, celesta, organ, four brass bands, two huge double choirs and four vocal soloists. The work gave Brian great public success at its first professional performance in 1966, but has had the adverse effect of stereotyping him as an eccentric composer of massive, difficult-to-perform works.

— THE FIRST COMPLETELY ELECTRONIC — MOVIE SOUNDTRACK

Forbidden Planet (1956), written by husband and wife team Bebe and Louis Barron.

THE FIRST MUSIC SCORE — WRITTEN SPECIFICALLY FOR FILM —

The soundtrack to *L'assassinat du Duc de Guise* (André Calmettes), written in 1908 by Camille Saint-Saëns (1835–1921).

— THE ENGLISH HORN (COR ANGLAIS) —

The English horn is neither English nor a horn. It is a kind of tenor oboe descended from a Baroque instrument known as an oboe da caccia ('hunting oboe'). This instrument was frequently used as a substitute for the hunting horn ('cor' in French), and since early models were made in a curved shape, the French referred to it as a *cor anglé* ('bent horn'). Eventually, *anglé* ('bent') came to be confused with *anglais* ('English'), and thus the *cor anglais* (English horn) got its name.

— TEN GOLDEN RULES FOR A CONDUCTOR — (BY RICHARD STRAUSS)

As inscribed in *The Album Of A Young Conductor*, *circa* 1925:

'Remember that you are making music not to amuse yourself, but to delight your audience.'

'You should not perspire when conducting; only the audience should get warm.'

'Conduct *Salomé* and *Elektra* as if they were by Mendelssohn: elfin music.'

'Never look encouragingly at the brass, except with a brief glance to give an important cue.'

'Never let the horns and woodwinds out of your sight. If you can hear them at all, they are still too strong.'

'If you think that the brass is not blowing hard enough, tone it down another shade or two.'

'It is not enough that you yourself should hear every word the soloist sings. You should know it by heart anyway.'

'The audience must be able to follow without effort. If they do not understand the words, they will go to sleep.'

'Always accompany a singer in such a way that he can sing without effort.'

'When you think you have reached the limits of *prestissimo*, double the pace.'

'If you follow these rules carefully, you will, with your fine gifts and your great accomplishments, always be the darling of your listeners...'

— ARTISTS WHO PERFORMED AT WOODSTOCK —

Joan Baez – Arlo Guthrie – Tim Hardin – The Incredible String Band – Ravi Shankar – Richie Havens – Sly And The Family Stone – Bert Sommer – Sweetwater – Quill – Canned Heat – Creedence Clearwater Revival – Jefferson Airplane – The Who – The Grateful Dead – Keef Hartley – Blood, Sweat And Tears – Crosby, Stills And Nash (And Young) – Santana – The Jeff Beck Group (cancelled) – The Band – Ten Years After – Johnny Winter – Jimi Hendrix – Janis Joplin – Joe Cocker – Mountain – Melanie – Sha-Na-Na – John Sebastian – Country Joe McDonald And The Fish – The Paul Butterfield Blues Band

— THE ONLY PALINDROMIC HIT SONG — BY A PALINDROMIC ARTIST

'SOS' by Abba

— THE FIRST EVER MOBO WINNERS (1996) —

Best Dance	Baby D
Best Jazz	Courtney Pine
Best Gospel	New Colours
Best Hip-hop	Blak Twang
Best Jungle	Goldie
Best R&B	Mark Morrison
Best Reggae	Peter Hunningale
Best Video	Tupac
Best DJ	Trevor Nelson
Best International Act	The Fugees
Best Newcomer	Peace By Piece
Best International Single	The Fugees
Best Single	Gabrielle
Best Producer	Teddy Riley
Best Album	Goldie
Outstanding Contribution	Jazzie B
Lifetime Achievement	Lionel Richie
International Achievement	Seal

— RIAA TOP TEN BEST-SELLING ARTISTS —

Artist	Certified Units (In Millions)	Artist	Certified Units (In Millions)
Beatles, The	164.50	Joel, Billy	77.00
Led Zeppelin	105.00	Pink Floyd	73.50
Brooks, Garth	105.00	Streisand, Barbra	68.50
Presley, Elvis	102.00	John, Elton	64.50
Eagles	86.00	Aerosmith	63.50

— RAPPERS' REAL NAMES —

Vanilla Ice – *Robert Van Winkle*
Snoop Doggy Dogg – *Calvin Broadus*
Shaggy – *Orville Richard Burrell*
Tupac Shakur – *Lesane Crooks*
Guru – *Keith Elam*
Queen Latifah – *Dana Owens*
Shabba Ranks – *Rexton Rawlston Gordon*
Notorious BIG – *Christopher Wallace*
LL Cool J – *James Todd Smith*
Foxy Brown – *Inga Marchand*
Chuck D – *Carlton Douglas Ridenhour*
Coolio – *Artis Ivey*
Flavor Flav – *William Dreyton*
KRS One – *Kris Parker*
Eric B – *Eric Barrier*
Rakim – *William Griffin*
Timbaland – *Tim Mosely*
Missy Elliot – *Melissa Elliot*
Slick Rick – *Ricky Walters*
Redman – *Reggie Noble*
MC Hammer – *Stanley Kirk Burrell*
Ice T – *Tracy Marrow*
Grandmaster Flash – *Joseph Sadler*
Doug E Fresh – *Douglas Davies*

— MUSICIANS WHO HAVE APPEARED — IN *THE SIMPSONS*

Aerosmith • Sting • Spiñal Tap • Barry White • Red Hot Chili Peppers • James Brown • Paul and Linda McCartney • Paul Anka • Tony Bennet • Johnny Cash • U2 • David Crosby • The Who • Flea • Sonic Youth • George Harrison • Bob Hope • Tom Jones • Kid Rock • Cyndi Lauper • Bette Midler • Dolly Parton • Tito Puente • The Ramones • Britney Spears • Ringo Starr • Mick Jagger • Keith Richards • Lenny Kravitz • Larry Mullen • Elvis Costello

— STRAIGHT EDGE —

Straight Edge is a global movement connected with the punk/hardcore/metal scenes. The term is believed to have been coined by Ian Mackaye during his time with hardcore Washington band Minor Threat. Mackaye used the term 'Straight Edge' to denote a no-drugs/no-smoking/no-sex lifestyle as a reaction to the excesses of the rock scene. Some Straight Edgers are also vegetarians or vegans, and most seek to spread positive messages amongst society. The symbols below can be found on albums of Straight Edge groups and sometimes on the clothing and/or skin of Straight Edgers

Sxe
Xxx
X-x
X

— GUITAR TABLATURE —

)b – bend string up
| – ghost bend
Nh – natural harmonic
pm – palm mute
| – ghost bend and release
* – uncontrolled feedback
P – pull-off
R – release bend or reverse bend
X\x – pick scrape
/ – slide up
^ and **h** – hammer-on
**** – slide down
V – vibrato (sometimes written as ~)
T+ – right-hand tap
X – play note with heavy damping rhythm click or muted string
(5) – ghost note, or optional note
<5> – harmonic
S – slide (palm mute)

— GREGORIAN CHANTING —

Gregorian chanting is named after Pope Gregory the Great (*circa* AD 540–604), who ordered the standardisation of the entire religious chant repertoire. His idea was that the whole of Christian Europe should sing the same hymns. Since there was no form of musical notation at that time, he organised in Rome the Schola Cantorum, a school of singers who trained monks to memorise the chants in a uniform style. Towards the end of the eighth century, Emperor Charlemagne commissioned an authoritative anthology of the Gregorian chants and suppressed any regional chant 'dialects'. It is Charlemagne's collection that has been inherited – some believe that in fact the chanting should be called Carolingian chanting.

— THE BRILL BUILDING —

New York's famous Brill Building was named after clothing-store owners the Brill Brothers, who purchased the store in order to rent it out. The Depression meant a lack of wealthy professionals to rent the property to, so the brothers were more or less forced to rent the spaces to music publishers. By 1962 the building contained 165 music businesses, covering almost every aspect of the music industry. Some of the greatest songwriters of the '60s were based there, such as Gerry Goffin and Carole King, Neil Sedaka and Howard Greenfield, Barry Mann and Cynthia Weil, Doc Pomus and Mort Shuman, Jeff Barry and Ellie Greenwich, Jerry Leiber and Mike Stoller, and Burt Bacharach and Hal David, to name just a few.

TEN CLASSICS PENNED BY — JERRY LEIBER AND MIKE STOLLER —

Elvis Presley – 'Hound Dog' – RCA 1956
Michael McDonald – 'I Keep Forgettin' (Every Time You're Here)' – Warner Bros 1982
Elvis Presley – 'She's Not You' – RCA 1962
The Coasters – 'Charlie Brown' – Atco 1959
Aretha Franklin – 'Spanish Harlem' – Atlantic 1971
George Benson – 'On Broadway' – Warner Bros 1978
Ben E King – 'Stand By Me' – Atco 1961
The Coasters – 'Poison Ivy' – Arco 1959
The Searchers – 'Love Potion Number Nine' – Atco 1965
Peggy Lee – 'Is That All There Is' – Capitol 1969

— FORMER BANDNAMES —

The Beatles – *The Quarry Men*
Talking Heads – The *Vague Dots*
The Police – *Strontium 90*
Earth, Wind And Fire – *The Salty Peppers*
Culture Club – *Sex Gang Children*
Dire Straits – *The Café Racers*
The Beach Boys – *Carl And The Passions*
Abba – *The Engaged Couples*
The Spice Girls – *Touch*
The Bee Gees – *Wee Johnnie Hayes And The Bluecats*
Nirvana – *Fecal Matter*
U2 – *Feedback*
Radiohead – *On A Friday*
Led Zeppelin – *The New Yardbirds*
Blondie – *The Stilettos*
Depeche Mode – *Composition Of Sound*
Madness – *The Invaders*
Kajagoogoo – *Art Neauvou*
The Byrds – *The Beefeaters*
Marmalade – *Dean Ford And The Gaylords*
Status Quo – *The Spectres*
The Bee Gees – *The Rattlesnakes*
Oasis – *Rain*
Queen – *Smile*
Simon And Garfunkel – *Tom And Jerry*
Motörhead – *Bastard*
Wham! – *The Executive*
Teenage Fanclub – *The Boy Hairdressers*
Blur – *Seymour*

— A TOAST TO NELLIE —

Melba toast is named after the Australian opera singer Dame Nellie Melba (1861–1931).

— UKE CANNOT BE SERIOUS —

'Ukulele' means 'jumping flea' in Hawaiian, and refers to the fast movement of the player's fingers.

— PRESIDENTIAL PIANOS —

George Washington
Longman & Broderip harpsichord; Schoen & Vinsen pianoforte

John Adams
Currier & Co

Thomas Jefferson
Astor pianoforte

Martin Van Buren
Hallet & Cumston square piano

William Henry Harrison
Haines Brothers

John Tyler
Thomas Tomkinson upright piano

James Knox Polk
Astor & Harwood square piano

James Buchanan
Chickering grand piano

Abraham Lincoln
Chickering square piano and Chickering upright

Andrew Johnson
Steinway & Sons square piano

James A. Garfield
Hallet & Davis upright

Grover Cleavland
Combination piano and harpsichord

Benjamin Harrison
J & C Fischer upright piano, Haines Brothers square

Grover Cleveland
J & C Fischer upright piano, Haines Brothers square

William Mckinley
AH Gale Co square piano

Theodore Roosevelt
Chickering upright, Steinway grand piano

William Howard Taft
Baldwin grand piano

Woodrow Wilson
Ernst Rosenkranst square piano, Knabe grand

Warren G. Harding
AB Chase electric player piano

Calvin Coolidge
Sohmer upright piano

Herbert Hoover
Knabe grand and AB Chase grand

Franklin D Roosevelt
Hardman grand

Harry S Truman
Steinway grand, Baldwin grand and Steinway upright

Dwight D Eisenhower
Hallet & Cumston upright

John F Kennedy
Ivers & Pond grand piano

Lyndon B Johnson
Style L Steinway, Knabe console

Richard M Nixon
Geo. P Bent upright, Baldwin vertical

Gerald Ford
No personal piano

James (Jimmy) Carter
Ludden & Bates

Ronald Reagan
Steinway grand

George Bush
No personal piano

Bill Clinton
Baldwin grand in the Governor's Mansion.

— THE JACKSON 5 —

Jermaine, Michael, Tito, Jackie, Marlon

— TEN THINGS YOU POSSIBLY DIDN'T KNOW — ABOUT…MOZART

- In 1777 Mozart fell in love with Aloysia Weber. She rejected him, so he married her sister, Constanze Weber.
- Mozart was only five years old when he wrote the melody now sung to 'Twinkle, Twinkle, Little Star'.
- Mozart once composed a piano piece that required the player to use both hands and his nose in order to hit all the right notes.
- Four out of Mozart's six children lived less than six months.
- Mozart's sister, Maria Anna Nannerl, was also a musical child prodigy.
- Mozart was so poor when he died that he was buried in an unmarked pauper's grave in Vienna. His body has never been located.
- Mozart loved to play billiards, and would sometimes play all night, composing symphonies as he played.
- Friends and family called Mozart 'Wolfie'.
- Mozart wrote out the entire score of the sacred 'Miserere' by Allegri after only two hearings.
- At the age of two, Mozart identified a pig's squeal as being a G♯.

— ANAGRAMMATIC ARTISTS —

Britney Spears – Best PR In Years
Jim Morrison – Mr Mojo Risin
Barry Manilow – Worry, I'm Banal
Axl Rose – Oral Sex
Belinda Carlisle – Ideal Braincells
Bruce Springsteen – Bursting Presence
Claude Debussy – Busy Scale Dude
David Lee Roth – Hot Daredevil
Elvis Aaron Presley – Seen Alive? Sorry, Pal
James Taylor – Oral Majesty

James Brown – Mr Jawbones
The Beatles – The Able Set
Sir Paul McCartney – Musical Carpentry
Carlos Santana – Carnal Sonatas
Dolly Parton – Party On, Doll
George Harrison – Gregorian Horse
Little Richard – A Direct Thrill

— HOW TO CIRCULAR BREATHE —

- Fill your mouth full of air and puff your cheeks out, holding the air.
- Breathe in and out through your nose.
- Still holding the air in your cheeks, empty your lungs through your nose.
- Now slowly breathe in through your nose and simultaneously push the air out of your mouth with your cheeks.
- Breathe out of your mouth, keeping your cheeks puffed.
- Breathe in through your nose, expelling the air from your cheeks.
- Breathe out, keep cheeks puffed.
- Continue this cycle until it's continuous.

— TEN THINGS YOU POSSIBLY DIDN'T KNOW — ABOUT...MICHAEL JACKSON

- Michael allegedly used to go to Disneyland in a wheelchair so that he could get on the rides first.
- Michael allegedly used to keep six mannequins in his room and dress them in evening gowns and boas and talk to them.
- Michael owns the rights to the South Carolina state anthem.
- Michael was paid $15 million to appear in two commercials.

— TEN THINGS YOU POSSIBLY DIDN'T KNOW — ABOUT...MICHAEL JACKSON (CONT'D)

- Michael was the seventh in a family of nine children.
- As a child, Michael was nicknamed 'big nose' by his father.
- After allegedly lightening his skin, Michael blamed it on vitiligo, a condition that causes pigment-lacking patches of skin on people of colour.
- Michael's first paying gig was for $7 at a place called 'Mr Lucky's Lounge'.
- Michael had performed in several strip clubs by the age of six.
- Michael has been involved in over 1,500 law suits.

— AULD LANG SYNE —

The song that everybody knows but nobody knows the words to, 'Auld Lang Syne's lyrics were adapted by Robert Burns (1759–1796) from a traditional Scotch song. The title means 'old long ago', or 'the good old days'.

(Scottish Version)
Should auld acquaintance be forgot,
And never brought to mind?
Should auld acquaintance be forgot,
And days o' lang syne!

Chorus:
For auld lang syne, my dear
For auld lang syne,
We'll tak a cup o' kindness yet
For auld lang syne!

We twa hae run about the braes,
And pu'd the gowans fine,
But we've wander'd mony a weary foot
Sin' auld lang syne.

We twa hae paidl't in the burn
Frae morning sun till dine,

But seas between us braid hae roar'd
Sin' auld lang syne.

And there's a hand, my trusty fiere,
And gie's a hand o' thine,
And we'll tak a right guid willie-waught
For auld lang syne!

And surely ye'll be your pint' stoup,
And surely I'll be mine!
And we'll tak a cup o' kindness yet
For auld lang syne!

Times Gone By
(English Version)

Should old acquaintances be forgotten,
And never brought to mind?
Should old acquaintances be forgotten,
And days of long ago!

Chorus:
For times gone by, my dear
For times gone by,
We will take a cup of kindness yet
For times gone by.

We two have run about the hillsides
And pulled the daisies fine,
But we have wandered many a weary foot
For times gone by.

We two have paddled (waded) in the stream
From noon until dinner time,
But seas between us broad have roared
Since times gone by.

And there is a hand, my trusty friend,
And give us a hand of yours,
And we will take a goodwill drink (of ale)
For times gone by!

And surely you will pay for your pint,
And surely I will pay for mine!
And we will take a cup of kindness yet
For times gone by!

— COUNTRY MUSIC HALL OF FAME INDUCTEES —

1961 Jimmie Rodgers
1961 Fred Rose
1961 Hank Williams
1962 Roy Acuff
1964 Tex Ritter
1965 Ernest Tubb
1966 Eddy Arnold
1966 James R Denny
1966 George D Hay
1966 Uncle Dave Macon
1967 Red Foley
1967 JL Frank
1967 Jim Reeves
1967 Stephen H Sholes
1968 Bob Wills
1969 Gene Autry
1970 Bill Monroe
1970 Original Carter Family
1971 Arthur Edward Satherley
1972 Jimmie H Davis
1973 Chet Atkins
1973 Patsy Cline
1974 Owen Bradley
1974 Frank 'Pee Wee' King
1975 Minnie Pearl
1976 Kitty Wells
1976 Paul Cohen
1977 Merle Travis
1978 Grandpa Jones
1979 Hubert Long
1979 Hank Snow
1980 Connie B Gay
1980 Original Sons Of The Pioneers
1980 Johnny Cash
1981 Vernon Dalhart
1981 Grant Turner
1982 Lefty Frizzell
1982 Marty Robbins
1982 Roy Horton
1983 Little Jimmy Dickens
1986 Whitey Ford
1987 Rod Brasfield
1988 Roy Rogers
1988 Loretta Lynn
1989 Cliffie Stone
1989 Hank Thompson
1989 Jack Stapp
1990 Tennessee Ernie Ford
1991 Felice And Boudleaux Bryant
1992 Frances Williams Preston
1992 George Jones
1993 Willie Nelson
1994 Merle Haggard
1995 Jo Walker-Meador
1995 Roger Miller
1996 Patsy Montana
1996 Buck Owens
1996 Ray Price
1997 Harlan Howard
1997 Brenda Lee
1997 Cindy Walker
1998 George Morgan
1998 Elvis Presley
1998 EW 'Bud' Wendell
1998 Tammy Wynette
1999 Johnny Bond
1999 Dolly Parton
1999 Conway Twitty
2000 Charley Pride
2000 Faron Young
2001 Bill Anderson
2001 The Delmore Brothers
2001 The Everly Brothers
2001 Don Gibson
2001 Homer And Jethro
2001 Waylon Jennings
2001 The Jordanaires
2001 Don Law
2001 The Louvin Brothers
2001 Ken Nelson

1984 Ralph S Peer
1984 Floyd Tillman
1985 Lester Flatt And Earl Scruggs
1986 Wesley H Rose
2001 Webb Pierce
2001 Sam Phillips
2002 Bill Carlisle
2002 Porter Wagoner

— ROBERT JOHNSON AND THE PACT WITH DEVIL —

Blues guitarist Robert Johnson was born in Hazelhurst, Mississippi, in 1911. Between 1936 and 1937, he recorded such immortal classics as 'I Believe I'll Dust My Broom', 'Sweet Home Chicago', 'Come On In My Kitchen', 'Crossroad Blues', 'Traveling Riverside Blues', 'Love In Vain', 'Hellhound On My Trail' and 'Me And The Devil Blues' – songs that have profoundly influenced many guitar players from Eric Clapton to Muddy Waters. In his recording of 'Crossroads Blues', Johnson tells of how he stood at a crossroads trying to hitch a ride. In Deep South mythology, the crossroads was where pacts were made with the Devil, and the dark nature of his material recorded after this song has led people to believe that Johnson's inimitable skills came out of a pact he made with Satan. Whether he really exchanged his soul for the ability to play better than anyone on the guitar is still a hotly contested issue. Johnson died under still-mysterious circumstances in Greenwood, Mississippi, in 1938. Some say he was murdered (poisoned). Others say the Devil merely called in the deal.

— METRONOME —

In 1696, Etieune Loulie made the first recorded attempt to apply the pendulum to a metronome. His machine was an adjustable pendulum with calibrations but without an escapement to keep it in motion. In 1812, Dietrik Nikolaus Winkel found that a double-weighted pendulum (with a weight on each side of the pivot) would beat low tempos, even when made of short length. Johann Nepenuk Maelzel appropriated Winkel's idea and in 1816 started manufacturing Maelzel's metronome. The device is in common use to this day and is still known by its original name. A notation on a musical score of 'mm = 80' informs the musician that the Maelzel metronome should be set to a rate of 80 beats per minute.

— OFFICIAL SONGS OF US STATES —

Alabama	*Alabama*
Alaska	*Alaska's Flag*
Arizona	*Arizona*
Arkansas	*Arkansas* and *Oh, Arkansas*
California	*I Love You, California*
Colorado	*Where The Columbines Grow*
Connecticut	*Yankee Doodle*
Delaware	*Our Delaware*
Florida	*Swanee River* and *Florida, My Florida*
Georgia	*Georgia On My Mind*
Hawaii	*Hawaii Ponoi*
Idaho	*Here We Have Idaho*
Illinois	*Illinois*
Indiana	*On The Banks Of The Wabash*
Iowa	*The Song Of Iowa*
Kansas	*Home On The Range*
Kentucky	*My Old Kentucky Home*
Louisiana	*Give Me Louisiana* and *You Are My Sunshine*
Maine	*State Song Of Maine*
Maryland	*Maryland My Maryland*
Massachusetts	*Hail Massachusetts*
Michigan	*Michigan, My Michigan*
Minnesota	*Hail! Minnesota*
Mississippi	*Go Mis-Sis-Sip-Pi*
Missouri	*Missouri Waltz*
Montana	*Montana* and *Montana Melody*
Nebraska	*Beautiful Nebraska*
Nevada	*Home Means Nevada*
New Hampshire	*Old New Hampshire*
New Jersey	*I'm From New Jersey*
New Mexico	*O, Fair New Mexico*
New York	*I Love New York*
North Carolina	*The Old North State*
North Dakota	*North Dakota Hymn*
Ohio	*Beautiful Ohio*
Oklahoma	*Oklahoma*
Oregon	*Oregon, My Oregon*
Pennsylvania	*Pennsylvania*

Rhode Island	*Rhode Island, It's For Me*
South Carolina	*Carolina*
South Dakota	*Hail, South Dakota*
Tennessee	*My Homeland Tennessee*; *When It's Iris Time In Tennessee*; *My Tennessee*; *The Tennessee Waltz*; *Rocky Top*; and *Tennessee*
Texas	*Texas, Our Texas*
Utah	*Utah, We Love Thee*
Vermont	*Hail, Vermont*
Virginia	*Carry Me Back To Old Virginia*
Washington	*Washington, My Home*
West Virginia	*The West Virginia Hills*; *This Is My West Virginia* and *West Virginia, My Home*
Wisconsin	*On Wisconsin*
Wyoming	*Wyoming*

THE WEDDING DAY MIXTAPE — (MUSIC TO GET MARRIED TO) —

'Baby I Love Your Way' – Peter Frampton
'Endless Love' – Lionel Richie And Diana Ross
'(Everything I Do) I Do It For You' – Bryan Adams
'Glory Of Love' (Love Theme from *The Karate Kid II*) – Peter Cetera
'I Will Always Love You' – Whitney Houston
'Tonight I Celebrate My Love' – Peabo Bryson And Roberta Flack
'The Wedding Song (There Is Love)' – Petula Clark
'Always' – Atlantic Starr
'The Wind Beneath My Wings' – Bette Midler
'Unchained Melody' – The Righteous Brothers
'Matrimony' – Gilbert O'Sullivan
'Every Breath You Take' – The Police
'Every Time You Go Away' – Paul Young
'Have I Told You Lately That I Love You' – Kenny Rogers
'Lady In Red' – Chris De Burgh
'My Heart Will Go On (Love Theme From *Titanic*)' – Celine Dion
'Unforgettable' – Nat 'King' Cole With Natalie Cole
'You're The Inspiration' – Chicago

— HOW TO PLAY THE MUSICAL SAW (STEP BY STEP) —

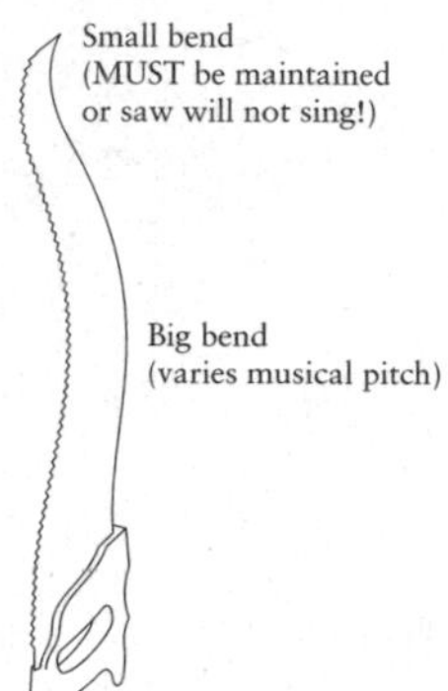

Sit in a straight-backed chair.
Hold saw in a vertical position, teeth facing you.

Clamp saw handle tightly between legs
Grab tip off saw with left hand and bend blade leftwards between 6" and 10".

Rotate left wrist clockwise to bend top
Bend saw into an 'S' shape

Place bow at right angle to flat surface in the centre and at right angles to edge.

Run bow slowly across the saw.
Change musical pitch by making big bend larger or smaller, while taking care to maintain the tip-bend

* *The saw will ideally have a blade length (measured along the teeth) of no less than 26" or 28".*

** *Musical saw manufacturers: Mussehl & Westphal, USA; Charlie Blacklock, California, USA; Sandvik, Sweden; Parkstone, England; Feldmann, Germany.*

— FORMER JOBS OF THE STARS —

Lou Reed	Accountant
George Michael	Cinema usher
Shane McGowan	Barman
James Brown	Shoeshine boy
Hugh Cornwall	Chemist
Cliff Richard	Credit-control clerk
Belinda Carlisle	Petrol-pump attendant
Julio Inglesias	Goalkeeper for Real Madrid
Björk	Fish-factory worker
Woody Guthrie	Drugstore clerk
Shania Twain	McDonald's employee
Jon Bon Jovi	Burger King employee
Captain Sensible	Toilet cleaner
Chubby Checker	Chicken plucker

Bryan Ferry	Ceramics teacher
Peter Gabriel	Travel agent
Bob Geldof	Hotdog vendor
Mick Jagger	Ice-cream seller and coat-room attendant
Madonna	Doughnut-shop employee
Van Morrisson	Window cleaner
Rod Stewart	Gravedigger/coffin polisher
Jah Wobble	Tube driver
Garth Brookes	Manager of Cowboy store
Queen Latifah	Burger King employee
Mariah Carey	Restaurant hostess
Elvis Costello	Computer operator at cosmetics factory
Frank Zappa	Greetings-card manufacturer
Jon Bon Jovi	Floor sweeper
Cindy Lauper	Dog-kennel cleaner
Jah Wobble	Tube driver
Sharleen Spiteri (Texas)	Hairdresser

— DOUBLE MEANING —

Schizophonia – from the Greek schizo ('split') and phone ('voice', 'sound'). The term was coined by Canadian composer RM Schafer to describe the split between an original sound and its electro-acoustic reproduction.

— PIANO SIZES —

Grand

Concert Grand – 8' and higher
Conservatory – 5' 4"–7' 11"
Studio – 5' 1"–5' 3"
Baby Grand – 5' and lower

Vertical

Upright – 49'–60'
Studio – 45'–48'
Console – 40'–43'
Spinet – 35'–39'

— TIMELINE OF THE DEVELOPMENT — OF RECORDED SOUND

1878 Phonograph and tin foil cylinders invented by Thomas Edison.

1881 Gramophone and discs invented by Emile Berliner, who also invents a system (electroplating) whereby records can be mass-produced.

1885 Graphophone invented by Alexander Bell and Charles Tainter.

1890 First 'jukebox' unveiled – a coin-operated cylinder phonograph with four listening tubes.

1890 Shellac replaces rubber in record manufacture.

1896 Eldridge Johnson releases his improved gramophone with a motor.

1898 Valdemar Poulsen patents the telegraphone, the first magnetic recorder using steel wire.

1902 Double-sided discs patented by Ademor Petit.

1909 The 'album' pioneered by Odeon.

1925 First electrically recorded discs and orthophonic phonographs on sale.

1929 Magnavox reduce loudspeaker hum.

1927 First coin-operated phonograph 'jukebox' presented by AMI.

1931 Alan Blumlein patents the 'binaural' (stereo) recording method in England.

1934 Rock-Ola, Seeburg and Wurlitzer introduce multiple-selection nickel jukeboxes.

1934 BASF manufacture reels of plastic-based tape.

1948 First 12", 33⅓rpm micro-groove LP vinyl record produced by Columbia.

1949 RCA Victor introduce 7", 45rpm micro-groove extended-play vinyl records.

1958 World standard for stereo records established.

1958 First stereo LPs sold.

1958 Koss introduce stereo headphones.

1963 Philips demonstrate first compact audio cassette.

1966 Cars equipped with eight-track stereo cartridge tape players (USA).

1969 Dolby noise reduction introduced for pre-recorded tapes.

1979 TPS-12 walkman portable audio cassette player introduced by Sony.

1982 First digital audio 5" CD discs marketed.

1985 Sony and Philips produce standard for compact disc read-only memory (CD-ROM).

1987 Digital audio tape (DAT) players introduced.

1997 MP3.com founded by Michael Robertson.

2001 Apple introduce the iPod portable music player.

— MUZAK —

The term 'muzak' tends to be associated today with passionless background music. The word was invented by general George Squier, who formed the Muzak Company in the USA after developing the idea of creating music for office environments as a means of increasing productivity. He named his business by merging the word *music* with his other favourite company, Kodak. Squier patented the transmission of background music – records played via phonographs over electrical lines – in the 1920s, and muzak became increasingly popular through the '20s and '30s, when the company started piping gentle music into the first elevators in America in order to soothe the fears of the people inside them. Today, the company is still going strong, pumping muzak into boutiques, food chains and offices all around the world. Approximately 90 million people listen to muzak daily.

— THE ACHEY-BREAKY HEART MIXTAPE — (MUSIC TO BREAK UP TO)

Joy Division – 'Love Will Tear Us Apart'
Abba – 'Winner Takes It All'
The Smiths – 'I Know It's Over'
Lou Reed – 'Sad Song'
Phil Collins – 'Against All Odds'
Patsy Cline – 'Crazy'
Serge Gainsbourg – 'Je Suis Venu Te Dire Que Je M'en Vais (I Came To Tell You I'm Leaving)'
Sinéad O'Connor – 'Nothing Compares 2 U'
Gloria Gaynor – 'I Will Survive'
Portishead – 'Numb'
Paul Simon – '50 Ways To Leave Your Lover'
Nina Simone – 'I Get Along Without You Very Well (Sometimes)'
Simply Red – 'If You Don't Know Me By Now'
Dionne Warwick – 'Walk On By'
Roxette – 'Must Have Been Love'
Richard Marx – 'Right Here Waiting For You'
The Wedding Present – 'What Have I Said Now?'
Toni Braxton – 'Un-break My Heart'
The Police – 'Every Breath You Take'
Heart – 'Alone'
Meat Loaf – 'Two Out Of Three Ain't Bad'
Smokey Robinson And The Miracles – 'The Tracks Of My Tears'
Inspiral Carpets – 'This Is How It Feels'

— THE COCKTAIL-PARTY EFFECT —

A term used to describe the ability in perception to select one desired sound from a background of ambient noise heard at the same time.

— JAMMIN' —

The Longest Mass-Guitar Jam Ever was arranged by Randy Bachman (former guitarist for Bachman-Turner Overdrive). He assembled more than 1,300 guitarists in Vancouver in 1994 to perform a 68-minute version of BTO's 'Takin' Care Of Business'.

— NOTE VALUES AND THEIR SIGNS —

English	American	Italian	French	German	Sign	Rest
breve	double whole note	breve	carrée (square)	Doppeltaktnote	𝅜	𝄺
Number equal to semibreve: 0.5						
semibreve	whole note	semibreve (round)	ronde	Ganze Taktnote	𝅝	𝄻
Number equal to semibreve: 1						
minim	half note	minima bianca	blanche (white)	Halbe/Halbenote/ Halbe Taktnote	𝅗𝅥	𝄼
Number equal to semibreve: 2						
crotchet	quarter note	semiminima nera	noire (black)	Viertel	♩	𝄽 or 𝄾
Number equal to semibreve: 4						
quaver	eighth note	croma	croche (hook)	Achtel	♪	𝄾
Number equal to semibreve: 8						
semiquaver	16th note	semicroma	double-croche (double hook)	Sechzehntel	𝅘𝅥𝅯	𝄿
Number equal to semibreve: 16						
demisemi-quaver	32nd note	biscroma	triple-croche (triple hook)	Zweiund-dreissigstel	𝅘𝅥𝅰	𝅀
Number equal to semibreve: 32						
hemidemi-semiquaver	64th note	semi-biscroma	quadruple-croche (quadruple hook)	vierundsech-zigstel	𝅘𝅥𝅱	𝅁
Number equal to semibreve: 64						
rest	rest	pausa	silence/pause	pause		

— THE 'DO-RE-MI' SCALE —

Immortalised forever in the movie *The Sound Of Music,* the do-re-mi scale was invented many centuries ago by a monk named Guido d'Arezzo. Guido invented modern musical notation (ie staff notation) and consequently observed the need for singers to identify the intervals between notes. To make the scale memorable for his students, he employed the initial syllables of a well-known hymn to St John The Baptist – 'Ut Queant Laxis'. Later on, the 'Ut' was changed to 'Do', although 'Ut' is still used in France. 'Tee' was added at the top of the scale.

Ut queant laxis
Resonare fibris
Mira gestorum
Famuli tuorum
Solve polluti
Labii reatum

— CAMEOS —

Rick Wakeman, *Mellotron* – David Bowie's 'A Space Oddity'
Elton John, *Piano* – The Hollies' 'He Ain't Heavy, He's My Brother'
George Harrison, *Guitar* – Cream's 'Badge'
Dave Gilmour, *Guitar* – Kate Bush's 'Wuthering Heights'
Mark King, *Bass* – Midge Ure's 'If I Was'
Sting, *Vocals* – Dire Straits' 'Money For Nothing'
Herb Alpert, *Trumpet* – UB40's 'Rat In Me Kitchen'
John Lennon, *Backing Vocals* – David Bowie's 'Fame'
Mick Jagger, *Backing Vocals* – Carly Simon's 'You're So Vain'
Jeff Beck, *Guitar* – Tina Turner's 'Private Dancer'
The Average White Band, *Backing Band* – Chuck Berry's 'My Ding-A-Ling'
Bono, *Guitar* – Roy Orbison's 'She A Mystery To Me'
Kate Bush, *Backing Vocals* – Peter Gabriel's 'Games Without Frontiers'
Ray Charles, *Handclaps* – The Archies' 'Sugar Sugar'
Cher, *Backing Vocals* – The Crystals' 'Da Doo Ron Ron'
Bootsy Collins, *Bass* – James Brown's 'Get Up'
Phil Collins, *Drums* – Adam Ant's 'Puss In Boots'
Donovan, *Backing Vocals* – The Beatles' 'Yellow Submarine'
Bob Dylan, *Vocals* – U2's 'Love Rescue Me'
Holly Johnson (Frankie Goes To Hollywood), *Backing Vocals* – ABC's 'SOS'
Michael Jackson, *Backing Vocals* – Rockwell's 'Somebody's Watching Me'
Billy Joel, *Piano* – The Shangri-Las' 'Leader Of The Pack'
Chaka Khan, *Backing Vocals* – Robert Palmer's 'Addicted To Love'
Luther Vandross, *Backing Vocals* – Chic's 'Le Freak'
Stevie Wonder, *Harmonica* – Chaka Khan's 'I Feel For You'
Kirsty MacColl, *Backing Vocals* – The Happy Mondays' 'Hallelujah' and The Smiths' 'Hand In Glove'
Paul Weller, *Guitar* – Oasis's 'Champagne Supernova'

— CASTRATI —

As the name suggests, Castrati were boys who were castrated in order to preserve their singing voices. The practice was ostensibly illegal, but since most of the boys came from poor families, ways around the law were found by parents who saw it as a route out of poverty – 'accidental' injuries were rife. The standard castration procedure involved drugging the boy with opium, putting him in warm water until he became unconscious and then severing the ducts leading to the testes. Not all the boys recovered, but those who did were used for church singing. It is estimated that, at the height of the castratis' popularity, during the 18th century, as many as 4,000 boys a year were being castrated in Italy; the Vatican even used them in the Sistine Chapel. Very few castrati became rich but some achieved a modicum of fame. The last known castrato, Alessandro Moreschi, died in 1922. He was the director of the Sistine Chapel Choir in Rome at St Peter's, and their soloist. One of the greatest castrato's was Farinelli, aka Carlo Broschi, who had a voice that allegedly spanned over three octaves.

—SOME EXHIBITS FROM THE ROCK AND ROLL — HALL OF FAME (OHIO, USA)

No. 88 Chuck Berry's Gibson ES-335 electric guitar.

No. 125 James Brown's tuxedo stage jacket, 1983.

No. 562 Little Richard's black jacket with appliqués.

No. 5338 Fats Domino's shirt.

No. 84 The Everly Brothers' suits.

No. 0495 Hank Williams' white wool felt cowboy hat.

No. 570 Ricky Nelson's Life Magazine cover.

No. 46 The Beatles' tabletop promotional display for Parlophone records, 1963.

No. 124 Otis Redding plane part, 1967.

No. 563 Lavern Baker's blue and white beaded dress.

No 43 'The Byrds Are Coming' poster.

No. 569 Doc Pomus's little saxophone.

No. 114 Al Green's white leather jacket with embroidery.

No. 464 Neil Young's fringed leather jacket.

No. 28 David Bowie's red-vinyl platform boots, 1970s.

No. 498 Paul Simonon (The Clash) 1979 Fender Precision electric bass guitar.

— *LA MUETTE DE PORTICI* —

La Muette de Portici is a 'freedom opera' by Daniel Auber. An epic tale about rebellious Neapolitan fishermen, its powerful messages of liberation were soon tested to the fullest at its opening performance in Belgium on 25 August 1830, when the audience were so stirred by the duet 'Amour sacré de la patrie' ('The holy love of the motherland') – which called for the casting off of foreign oppression – that they swept out of the theatre and began rioting. The revolt sparked similar riots in the provinces, and after some fighting, the Dutch colonists withdrew and national independence was proclaimed on 4 October 1830. The theatre still stands today as a permanent reminder to the Belgians of the moment of their liberation.

— GREEK MODES —

Aeolian Mode • Dorian Mode • Ionian Mode • Lydian Mode
Mixolydian Mode • Phrygian Mode • Syntolydian Mode

— I'VE GOT A LOVELY BUNCH OF COCONUTS —

Song/Lyrics: Fred Heatherton 1944,
Recorded and Performed by Danny Kaye

Down at an English fair one evening I was there,
When I heard a showman shouting underneath the flair:
I've got a lovely bunch of coconuts,
There they are all standing in a row,
Big ones, small ones, some as big as your head,
Give them a twist a flick of the wrist,
That's what the showman said .
I've got a lovely bunch of coconuts,
Every ball you throw will make me rich,
There stands my wife, the idol of me life,
Singing roll a bowl a ball a penny a pitch.
Roll a bowl a ball a penny a pitch,
Roll a bowl a ball a penny a pitch,
Roll a bowl a ball, roll a bowl a ball,
Singing roll a bowl a ball a penny a pitch.
I've got a lovely bunch of coconuts (they're lovely),
There they are all standing in a row (one, two, three, four),
Big ones, small ones, some as big as your head (and bigger),

Give them a twist a flick of the wrist,
That's what the showman said.
I've got a lovely bunch of coconuts,
Every ball you throw will make me rich,
There stands my wife, the idol of me life,
Singing roll a bowl a ball a penny a pitch (all together now),
Roll a bowl a ball a penny a pitch (harmony)
Roll a bowl a ball a penny a pitch
Roll a bowl a ball, roll a bowl a ball
Singing roll a bowl a ball a penny a pitch.

— BUNCH OF ARSE —

The Pogues' name is a shortening of *pogue mo chone* – Gaelic for 'kiss my arse'.

— BEAT THE CLOCK—

The most single-stroke drumbeats played in one minute is 1,026, achieved by the American Johnny Rabb on 28 April 2000 at the Nashville Music Institute, Nashville, Tennessee.

— THE NUMEROUS MONIKERS OF MR JAMES BROWN —

Minister Of The New, New Super-Heavy Funk
Hardest Working Man In Showbusiness
Forefather Of Hip-Hop
Soul Brother Number One
Original Disco Man
Real Black Moses
Ambassador Of Soul
Godfather Of Soul
Black Caesar
Funky President
Mister Star Time
Mister Dynamite

— IRA GERSHWIN'S FIVE Bs OF MUSIC —

Beethoven • Brahms • Berlin • Bach • Bacharach

— GOLD RECORDS —

When Glenn Miller sold over a million records of his song 'Chattanooga Choo-Choo' (recorded for the movie *Sun Valley Serenade*) in less than three months, his label (RCA Victor) decided to celebrate. Without telling Miller, they organised a publicity stunt whereby they lacquered a record gold and handed it to him during a live radio show on 10 February 1942. A decade later, the RIAA (Recording Industry Association of America) trademarked the gold record as a way of rewarding singles that had sold one million copies, or albums that had made over $1 million in sales. The first RIAA gold single was Perry Como's 'Catch A Falling Star', while the first RIAA gold album was Gordon McRae's soundtrack to *Oklahoma!*.

— LEVELS OF GOLD RECORD CERTIFICATION IN — DIFFERENT COUNTRIES

USA	500,000
France	250,000
Japan	200,000
UK	100,000
Italy	50,000
Thailand	50,000
Sweden	40,000
Australia	35,000
Hong Kong	25,000
Finland	20,000
Zimbabwe	10,000
Latvia	8,000
Ireland	7,500
Bolivia	5,000
Jamaica	5,000
Uruguay	3,000

— ARTISTS INVOLVED IN USA FOR AFRICA'S — 'WE ARE THE WORLD'

Lionel Richie • Michael Jackson • Harry Belafonte • Ray Charles • Lindsay Buckingham • James Ingram • Dan Ackroyd • Kim Carnes • Sheila E • Jackie, Latoya, Randy, Marlon and Tito Jackson (of The Jacksons) • Daryll Hall and John Oates • Bob Dylan • Al Jarreau • Cyndi Lauper • Kenny Loggins • Tina Turner • Huey Lewis And The News • Willie Nelson • Jeffrey Osbourne • Billy Joel • Waylon Jennings • Bette Midler • Steve Perry • Dionne Warwick • The Pointer Sisters • Stevie Wonder • Smokey Robinson • Kenny Rogers • Paul Simon • Diana Ross • Bruce Springsteen • Bob Geldof

— THE LONGEST NOTE HELD ON RECORD —

Morten Harket of the Norwegian band A-Ha held a vocal note for 20.2 seconds on their 2000 song 'Summer Moved On'. The longest note held on a solo single was sung by Bill Withers on 'Lovely Day', lasting 18 seconds.

— RIDE THE WAVE —

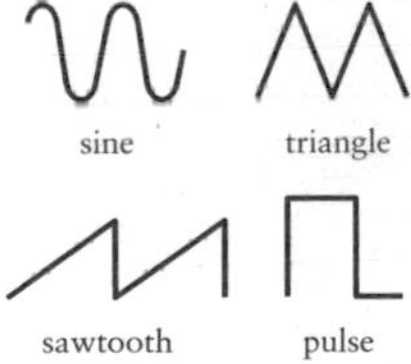

Cymatics (from the Greek *kyma*, meaning 'wave') is the 'science' of transforming sound into shapes developed by Swiss doctor and natural scientist Hans Jenny (1904–1972). Jenny's experiments involved using vibrations to activate inert powders, pastes and liquids into fluid and flowing forms. All of his patterns were created using simple sine-wave vibrations (pure tones) within the audible range to create physical representation of vibration. Jenny maintained that biological evolution was a result of vibrations, and aimed to produce a method of understanding how to heal the body with the help of tones and how different frequencies influence genes, cells and various structures in the body. Intriguingly, the shapes that Jenny's experiments created often resemble the physical environment around us – for example, in nature, art and architecture.

— A TASTE OF TOMATIS —

The Tomatis method refers to the work of Dr Alfred A Tomatis, an ear, nose and throat specialist born in France. His method – aka 'auditory training', 'auditory stimulation' and 'listening therapy' – is intended to re-educate the way we listen to improve learning and language abilities, communication, creativity and social behaviour. Perhaps the most poignant aspect of his theory, though, is the Tomatis effect, which posits that we can vocalise only those sounds that we can hear. His groundbreaking research led Tomatis to the following conclusions:

The primary function of the ear is to convert sound waves to electrochemical impulses that charge the neocortex of the brain.

Sound is a nutrient; we can either charge or discharge the nervous system by the sounds we take in through both air and bone conduction.

There is a distinction between hearing and listening. The two are related, but distinct, processes. Hearing is passive; listening is active. This corresponds to the difference between seeing and looking. Listening and looking are active focusing processes.

The quality of an individual's listening ability will affect both spoken and written language development; listening ability also influences communication, thereby shaping the individual's social development, confidence, and self-image.

The active process of listening can be enhanced or refocused by auditory stimulation using musical and vocal sounds rich in high frequencies. This entails the use of filtered and enhanced audio tapes employing the music of Mozart and Gregorian chant.

Communication is a process that begins *in utero*. The unborn child hears as early as the fourth months after conception. Sound actually helps the foetus's brain and nervous system to grow.

— NEUMES —

The roots of our present day music notation system lie in the plain-chant sources of the ninth and tenth centuries. Plain-chant was first notated with *neumes*, small dots and squiggles possibly derived from accents used in the Latin language. The shapes represent single notes and groups of notes, and suggest – rather than precisely indicate – changes of pitch within the melody...

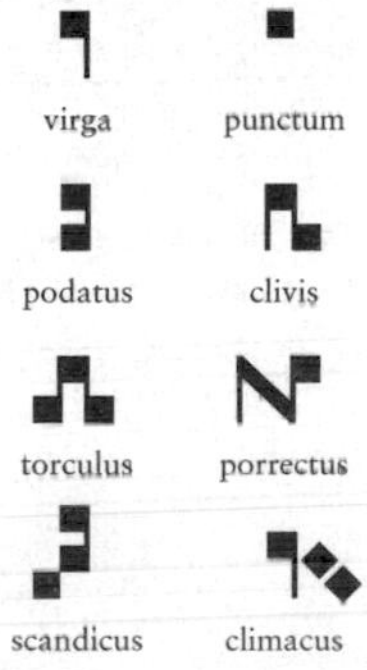

— I CAN HEAR A RAINBOW—

Synaesthesia – from the Greek *syn* meaning 'together' and *aisthesis*, meaning 'perception' – is a crossing or joining of the senses. Many synaesthesia sufferers see sound as colour and vice versa. Research has shown that at least one in every 25,000 people born have synaesthesia, and studies in the US and UK both show that women are between three and eight times more likely than men to be affected. Musicians such as Liszt, Messaien, Rimsky-Korsakov and Scriabin are all thought to have been sufferers. There are two types of synaesthesia: two-sensory and multiple-sensory. Neurologist Richard E Cytowic played a major role in rediscovering synaesthesia in the '70s. His five main diagnostic features are...

— I CAN HEAR A RAINBOW (CONTINUED) —

The sensations are involuntary: they cannot be suppressed or incurred, though the intensity is influenced by the situation in which they occur.

The sensations are projected into the environment: it is not just in the head; the person actually sees a sound or hears a picture, etc.

The sensations are durable and generic: every time you hear a bell, you always see red – it doesn't change over time or situation and will always be experienced with the stimulus.

The sensations are memorable: they are often the aspect of something that is remembered best. For example, it may be easier to remember that a person's name is yellow than the name, although the colour helps to recall the name.

The sensations are emotional: having this experience causes ecstasy and is viewed as an accomplishment.

* *The synaesthetic experience is different for every individual. There is no set colour for each letter from person to person – everyone has their own coloured alphabet.*

** *The first reference to synaesthesia is believed to have been in John Locke's 'Essay Concerning Human Understanding', where Locke recounted the story of a blind man who one day felt 'betrayed' when he learned what scarlet signified. When the blind man's friend asked what he had thought scarlet was, the blind man answered that it was 'like the sound of a trumpet'.*

ARTISTS INVOLVED IN BAND AID'S — 'DO THEY KNOW IT'S CHRISTMAS' —

Bob Geldof • Midge Ure • Phil Collins • Sting • Adam Clayton, Bono (from U2) • George Michael • Steve Norman • Christopher Cross • Duran Duran • Paul Young • Tony Hadley • Glenn Gregory • Jon Moss (of Culture Club) • Simon Crowe • Marilyn • Bananarama • Martin Kemp • Jody Watley • Paul Weller • James Taylor (of Kool And The Gang) • Martyn Ware • John Keeble • Gary Kemp

— HOCKET TO 'EM —

The Hocket technique is a practice of composition in which two voices move in such a manner that one is still while the other moves, and vice-versa. Sometimes this is achieved by taking a single melody and breaking it into short one- or two-note phrases and dividing the phrases between the two voices so that a quick back-and-forth movement of the melody can be heard. In music, a hocket is the interruption of a voice-part (usually of two or more parts alternately) by rests so as to produce a broken or spasmodic effect.

— NEHER RHYTHMIC DRUMMING TRANCES —

Andrew Neher, author of *Paranormal And Transcendental Experience*, developed a theory about the connection between the activity of drumming and stimulation of electrical impulses in the brain's neurons. He posits that drummers know intuitively the most potent brain-stimulating rhythms. According to Neher, the predominant drumming rhythm used in a number of African dances, as well as in Haitian Voodoo dances, is a fast seven to nine beats per second, which happens to be about the same rhythm produced naturally by brainwaves in the auditory cortex itself – ie groups of neurons charging and discharging in electrical unison. His conclusion is that properly synchronised drumbeats drive the brain and can force it into heightened activity.

THE OFFICIAL INSTRUMENTATION FOR — A BRASS BAND UNDER BRITISH LAW ALLOWS: —

1 E♭ Soprano Cornet
2 Euphoniums
1 B♭ Flugel Horn
3 E♭ Tenor Horns
2 B♭ Baritones (Small Bore)
2 B♭ Tenor Trombones (Small Bore)
9 B♭ Cornets
1 Bass Trombone (Big Bore)
2 E♭ Basses
2 B♭ Basses
3 Percussionists

— SNAKE CHARMING —

Most snake charmers are Bengali immigrants to the north Indian state of Uttar Pradesh. Snake charming itself is a profession that has been passed down the generations from back into the 17th century, though the practice is said to be endangered since the current generation of youth is eschewing the old music in favour of the songs popularised in Bollywood. The instrument used for the 'charming' is called a pungi. Cobras don't hear music as such; they feel the vibrations of the flute, though they don't physically respond to these vibrations, as is commonly thought. Rather, they respond to the actual movement of the instrument – the pose of the 'charmed' cobra is in fact a defensive posture. Many cobras strike the flute (rather than the flautist), but because this hurts the snake, it rarely strikes twice, preferring instead to puff up to it in a naturally on-guard posture.

— SMASHING PARTY TRICK —

To shatter a wine glass with your voice, you must match the natural frequency of the glass itself, thereby producing resonance with it. The glass shatters when the matching resonance created by the voice is produced at an amplitude that has grown greater than the natural amplitude of the glass. In early attempts at recording vocal music, particularly powerful voices inadvertently shattered the glass diaphragms used by technicians on the recording equipment. It generally requires a matching resonant tone to be maintained for 30 seconds to break a glass. Many classical and jazz vocalists are famous for breaking them, but it is within the means of anyone to do so. Heavy-metal band Nitro got signed to a major label on their first visit to LA when their vocalist shattered a glass – as he billed he would – before a sold-out show in Hollywood.

— PAISTE SOUND CREATION GONGS —

Sound creation gongs are the familiar 'gong' instrument, constructed individually to access individual tones specifically reflective of the underlying elements of the living universe. While these instruments reference the religious Buddhist temple gongs, they are primarily used in Western performance and recording.

SUN and MOON gongs – light for sun and darker harmonic tones for moon.

FIRE and WATER gongs – warm/ascending for fire and cool/soothing tones for water.

PEACE and FIGHT tones – harmonious secondary tones for peace and conflicting harmonics in fight.

— RENAISSANCE INSTRUMENTS —

Bladder Pipe	Pipe and Tabor	Rackett
Cornamuse	Psaltery	Recorder
Dulcian	Hurdy-Gurdy	Schalmei
Dulcimer	Crumhorn	Hirtenscalmei
Gamba	Viol	Transverse Flute
Harpsichord	Serpent	Zink
	Mute Cornett	

— ALEXANDER SCRIABIN'S 'MYSTIC CHORD' — OF FOURTHS

Also known as the 'Prometheus chord', Scriabin's mystic chord consists of a series of fourths: C, F♯, B♭, A, E and D). Scriabin attempted to compose entire pieces upon this chord, as it evolved to become the foundation for his entire musical language. Scriabin's 'Prometheus' is the foremost example of the power of the mystic chord – it is the seed from which the entire piece grows, and the piece has been described as a 'giant suspension of 1,000 discords and dissonant harmonies'. Scriabin, with a friend, developed a 'colour organ' that would project the various colours he would see when hearing various pitches, a condition known as *synaesthesia*.

— VIOLIN FACTS —

- Violins are the most numerous instruments in an orchestra.
- Violins are usually made of at least 70 different parts.
- Violin bows are made of real or synthetic horsehair.
- The proper relative humidity in which to store a violin is 45–55 degrees.
- A violin's fingerboard is traditionally made of ebony.
- Most violins are made from cut wood that has aged eight to ten years.
- The Italian name for the violin's sound post is *amina*, meaning 'soul'.
- A violin's scroll has no real purpose.
- Apprentices to Renaissance Italian violin makers had to take oaths swearing that they would not divulge the secrets of concocting varnish.
- The world record price paid for a Stradivarius at auction is $947,500 (£650,000).

— SOME UKRANIAN COMPOSERS —

Alexander Zlotnik
Mykola Lysenko
Alexander Sparinsky
Alexander Grinberg
Maksym Berezovsky
Alexander Shchetynsky
NV Lysenko
Igor Bilozir
Hryhory Veriovka
Karmella Tsepkolenko
Valentin Silvestrov

— TYPES OF COUNTERPOINT —

Counterpoint – the ability to musically say two things at once (aka polyphony).

Strict (aka student's counterpoint)
Double
Triple
Linear
Invertible
Quadruple
Florid
Imitative
Free (aka composer's counterpoint)
Combined

— TEN CLASSICS PRODUCED BY QUINCY JONES —

Michael Jackson	'Billie Jean'	Epic	1983
USA For Africa	'We Are The World'	Columbia	1985
George Benson	'Give Me The Night'	Warner Bros	1980
Brothers Johnson	'Strawberry Letter 23'	A&M	1977
Aretha Franklin	'Angel'	Atlantic	1973
Michael Jackson	'Thriller'	Epic	1984
Donna Summer	'Love Is In Control'	Geffen	1982
James Ingram And Michael McDonald	'Yah Mo B There'	Qwest	1984
Lesley Gore	'You Don't Own Me'	Mercury	1964
Patti Austin And James Ingram	'Baby, Come To Me'	Qwest	1983

— LINING OUT OR DEACONING —

...is when each line of a hymn is read out before the congregation sing it. This practice can be traced as far back as Moses (Exodus 15:20, 21: 'Moses led the psalm, and gave it out for the men, and then Miriam for the women') but was re-introduced in the mid-1600s with the advent of metric psalms for the benefit of those in the congregation who could not read. It is still in use in some parts of the world. The procedure has been memorably described by one critic as 'praising God by piecemeal'.

— NUMBERS OF PLAYERS —

One Player – Solo
Two Players – Duet
Three Players – Trio
Four Players – Quartet
Five Players – Quintet
Six Players – Sextet
Seven Players – Septet
Eight Players – Octet
Nine Players – Nonet
Ten Players – Dectet
Eleven Players – Undectet
Twelve Players – Duodectet

— PEOPLE WITH PERFECT PITCH —

Perfect pitch: the relatively rare ability to name a note on hearing it, or singing any note asked for.

Bach
Beethoven
Mozart
Chopin
Frank Sinatra
Leonard Bernstein
Barbara Streisand
Julie Andrews
Andre Previn
Stevie Wonder
Nat 'King' Cole
Miles Davis
Ella Fitzgerald
Glenn Gould
Yngwie Malmsteen
Eric Johnson
Tommy Mars
Bela Bartók
Jascha Heifetz
Paul Shaffer
Yo-Yo Ma
Joe Mennonna
Shakira
Vivaldi
Rimsky-Korsakov
Milt Jackson

— PATTER SONGS —

Patter songs are songs that fit the greatest number of words into the shortest amount of time. They are characterised by fast, short lines whose words are strung together more for the sake of sound than meaning. A patter song is not just any song that is spoken, because that is often the choice of the performer. Some examples:

'Major General's Song' (Gilbert And Sullivan)
'Trouble' (Meredith Willson)
'Without Me' (Eminem)
'Nightmare Song' (Gilbert And Sullivan)

'I've Got A Little List' (Gilbert And Sullivan)
'Mad Dogs And Englishmen' (Noël Coward)
'When I Was A Lad' (Gilbert And Sullivan)

— SCOTCH SNAPS —

An ornament so often used in Scottish music that its presence practically ensures the Scottish origin of the tune. It consists of a short note immediately followed by a longer one, or vice versa.

THE TORCH-SONG MIXTAPE — (MUSIC TO LOVE SOMEONE UNREQUITEDLY TO) —

The phrase 'to carry a torch' means to suffer an unrequited love – to continue to love and pine for someone long after the object of affection has gone. By 1934, romantic ballads of lost love and broken hearts were called 'torch songs', and many female nightclub singers who made them their speciality were known as 'torch singers'.

- 'Goodbye, Little Dream, Goodbye' – Cole Porter, 1936
- 'All Alone' – Irving Berlin, 1924
- 'Just One More Chance' – Sam Coslow and Arthur Johnston, 1931
- 'In The Wee Small Hours Of The Morning' – Bob Hilliard and David Mann, 1955
- 'Cry Me A River' – Arthur Hamilton, 1953
- 'Ev'ry Time We Say Goodbye' – Cole Porter, 1944
- 'Glad To Be Unhappy' – Lorenz Hart and Richard Rodgers, 1936
- 'How About Me?' – Irving Berlin, 1928
- 'I Left My Heart In San Francisco' – Douglass Cross And George Cory, 1954
- 'Ill Wind (You're Blowin' Me No Good)' – Ted Koehler and Harold Arlen, 1934

THE TORCH-SONG MIXTAPE (MUSIC TO LOVE — SOMEONE UNREQUITEDLY TO) (CONTINUED) —

- 'In A Sentimental Mood' – Duke Ellington, Irving Mills and Manny Kurtz, 1935
- 'Lover, Come Back To Me' – Oscar Hammerstein II and Sigmund Romberg, 1928
- 'Love Me Or Leave Me' – Gus Kahn and Walter Donaldson, 1928
- 'More Than You Know' – William Rose, Edward Eliscu and Vincent Youmans, 1929
- 'My Foolish Heart' — Ned Washington and Victor Young, 1949
- 'My Silent Love' – Edward Heyman and Dana Suesse, 1932
- 'My Old Flame' – Arthur Johnston and Sam Coslow, 1934
- 'Nobody's Heart' – From musical production *By Jupiter*, written by Lorenz Hart and Richard Rodgers, 1942
- ''Round Midnight' – Bernie Hanighen, Thelonious Monk and Cootie Williams, 1944
- 'Stormy Weather (Keeps Rainin' All The Time)' – Ted Koehler and Harold Arlen, 1933

— ORCHESTRAL INSTRUMENT FAMILIES —

Brass
Trumpet, Horn, Trombone, Baritone, Tuba

Strings
Violin, Viola, Cello, Bass

Woodwinds
Flute, Oboe, English Horn, Clarinet, Bassoon

Other
Percussion, Bells, Tympani, Harp, Harpsichord, Classical Piano

— CAMPTOWN RACES —

Stephen C Foster (1850)

De Camptown ladies sing dis song,
Doo-dah! Doo-dah!
De Camptown race track five miles long,
Oh! Doo-dah day!
I come down dah wid my hat caved in,
Doo-dah! Doo-dah!
I go back home wid a pocket full of tin,
Oh! Doo-dah day!

Chorus: Gwine to run all night!
Gwine to run all day!
I'll bet my money on de bob-tail nag,
Somebody bet on the bay.

De longtail filly and de big black hoss,
Doo-dah! Doo-dah!
Dey fly de track and dey both cut across,
Oh! Doo-dah day!
De blind hoss stick'n in a big mud hole,
Doo-dah! Doo-dah!
Can't touch the bottom wid a ten-foot pole,
Oh! Doo-dah day!

Chorus:

Old muley cow come on de track,
Doo-dah! Doo-dah!
De bob-tail flung her ober his back,
Oh! Doo-dah day!
Den fly along like a railroad car,
Doo-dah! Doo-dah!
And run a race with a shootin' star,
Oh! Doo-dah day!

Chorus:

See dem flyin' on a ten-mile heat,
Doo-dah! Doo-dah!
Round de race track, then repeat,
Oh! Doo-dah day!
I win my money on de bob-tail nag,
Doo-dah! Doo-dah!
I keep my money in an old tow bag,
Oh! Doo-dah day!

Chorus:

— A LIMITED BUT POTENTIALLY USEFUL — GLOSSARY OF TABLA TERMS

Bandish – a composition or fixed musical piece.
Brahma – God.
Chela – student.
Dadra – semi-classical style of singing.
Dholak masala – paste applied to inner surface of left-hand drum skin on some folk drums.
Geet – song.
Ghungharu – collection of tiny bells worn around the feet of a dancer.
Hathodi – small hammer used for tuning tablas.
Mahfil – a gathering, usually for poetry or music.
Matra – beat.
Mizrab – pick for playing sitar.
Namaskar – a greeting, or bringing together of the hands.
Pungi – snake charmer's instrument.
Riyaz – perseverance.
Swar – musical note.
Swarlipi – form of musical notation.
Tabaliya – a respectful term for a tabla player.
Ustad – a learned man, a master.

— BACH'S ART OF FUGUE —

Bach's final fugal pieces are unique in comparison to the multitude of fugal arrangements he composed throughout the rest of his career. The final pieces, referred to as 'The Art Of Fugue', are considered the definitive exploration of the form, despite the fact that the work trails off seemingly unfinished. In essence, the four-part fugue appears as a series of demonstrations of the fugal form itself, where, although each part is based around the same theme, the parts develop independently. Another fact that warrants the unique status of the piece is the spelling of his name (BACH) is woven into the musical notation at the end of the composition. Bach died shortly after writing the work.

— GLOBAL MARKET SHARES OF MAJOR LABELS —

	Polygram %	Sony %	Warner %	EMI %	BMG %	Market Value US $bn
Australia	13	27	18	18	6	0.7
Canada	20	13	24	10	8	1.1
US	13	14	22	10	12	12.1
Japan	13	18	7	14	8	7.6
Germany	23	12	13	22	15	3.3
UK	22	13	11	22	9	2.6
France	32	25	13	19	11	2.4
Holland	23	14	8	15	13	0.7
Italy	19	16	17	15	24	0.6
Korea	10	5	4	5	5	0.5
Sweden	20	19	13	26	22	0.3
Taiwan	17	5	13	6	5	0.3
World	13	13	14	16	14	35.5

— PULITZER PRIZE WINNERS —

(For years not listed, no award was made.)

1943 *Secular Cantata No. 2*, A Free Song, William Schuman
1944 *Symphony No. 4* (Op. 34), Howard Hanson
1945 *Appalachian Spring*, Aaron Copland
1946 *The Canticle Of The Sun*, Leo Sowerby
1947 *Symphony No. 3*, Charles Ives
1948 *Symphony No. 3*, Walter Piston
1949 *Louisiana Story Music*, Virgil Thomson
1950 *The Consul*, Gian Carlo Menotti
1951 Music for opera *Giants In The Earth*, Douglas Stuart Moore
1952 *Symphony Concertante*, Gail Kubik
1954 *Concerto For Two Pianos And Orchestra*, Quincy Porter
1955 *The Saint Of Bleecker Street*, Gian Carlo Menotti
1956 *Symphony No. 3*, Ernst Toch
1957 *Meditations On Ecclesiastes*, Norman Dello Joio
1958 *Vanessa*, Samuel Barber
1959 *Concerto For Piano And Orchestra*, John La Montaine
1960 *Second String Quartet*, Elliott Carter
1961 *Symphony No. 7*, Walter Piston

— PULITZER PRIZE WINNERS (CONTINUED) —

1962 *The Crucible*, Robert Ward
1963 *Piano Concerto No. 1*, Samuel Barber
1966 *Variations For Orchestra*, Leslie Bassett
1967 *Quartet No. 3*, Leon Kirchner
1968 *Echoes Of Time And The River*, George Crumb
1969 *String Quartet No. 3*, Karel Husa
1970 *Time's Encomium*, Charles Wuorinen
1971 *Synchronisms No. 6 For Piano And Electronic Sound*, Mario Davidowsky
1972 *Windows*, Jacob Druckman
1973 *String Quartet No. 3*, Elliott Carter
1974 *Notturno*, Donald Martino
1975 *From The Diary Of Virginia Woolf*, Dominick Argento
1976 *Air Music*, Ned Rorem
1977 *Visions Of Terror And Wonder*, Richard Wernick
1978 *Déjà Vu For Percussion Quartet And Orchestra*, Michael Colgrass
1979 *Aftertones Of Infinity*, Joseph Schwantner
1980 *In Memory Of A Summer Day*, David Del Tredici
1982 *Concerto For Orchestra*, Roger Sessions
1983 *Three Movements For Orchestra*, Ellen T Zwilich
1984 *Canti Del Sole*, Bernard Rands
1985 *Symphony Riverrun*, Stephen Albert
1986 *Wind Quintet IV*, George Perle
1987 *The Flight Into Egypt*, John Harbison
1988 *12 New Etudes For Piano*, William Bolcom
1989 *Whispers Out Of Time*, Roger Reynolds
1990 *Duplicates: A Concerto For Two Pianos And Orchestra*, Mel Powell
1991 *Symphony*, Shulamit Ran
1992 *The Face Of The Night, The Heart Of The Dark*, Wayne Peterson
1993 *Trombone Concerto*, Christopher Rouse
1994 *Of Reminiscences And Reflections*, Gunther Schuller
1995 *Stringmusic*, Morton Gould
1996 *Lilacs*, George Walker
1997 *Blood On The Field*, Wynton Marsalis
1998 *String Quartet* No. 2, Musica Instrumentalis, Aaron Jay Kernis
1999 *Concerto For Flute, Strings And Percussion*, Melinda Wagner

2000 *Life Is A Dream*, Opera In Three Acts: Act II, Concert Version, Lewis Spratlan
2001 *Symphony No. 2 For String Orchestra*, John Corigliano
2002 *Ice Field*, Harry Brant
2003 *On The Transmigration Of Souls*, John Adams

— PUFF THE MAGIC DRAGON —

Lyrics By Peter Yarrow and Leonard Lipton (1958), recorded by Peter, Paul And Mary (1963)

* *'Puff The Magic Dragon' was written by Leonard Lipton whilst waiting to meet his friend for dinner. His friend never showed up, but his friend's housemate, Peter Yarrow, did, and when he saw the poem he decided to compose some music for it. Later, Peter became one-third of the band Peter, Paul And Mary, who increasingly used the song in their live sets. Eventually it was recorded and made it to Number Two in the charts in 1963, prompting claims that the song was an allusion to narcotics rather than a homage to lost childhood innocence.*

Puff the magic dragon lived by the sea
And frolicked in the autumn mist in a land called Honalee.
Little Jackie Paper loved that rascal Puff
And brought him strings and sealing wax and other fancy stuff, Oh
Puff the magic dragon, lived by the sea
And frolicked in the autumn mist in a land called Honalee.
Puff the magic dragon, lived by the sea
And frolicked in the autumn mist in a land called Honalee

Together they would travel on a boat with billowed sail
Jackie kept a lookout perched on Puff's gigantic tail
Noble kings and princes would bow whene'er they came
Pirate ships would lower their flags when Puff roared out his name, Oh

Chorus:

A dragon lives forever, but not so little boys
Painted wings and giants's rings make way for other toys.
One grey night it happened, Jackie Paper came no more
And Puff that mighty dragon, he ceased his fearless roar.

— PUFF THE MAGIC DRAGON (CONTINUED) —

His head was bent in sorrow, green scales fell like rain
Puff no longer went to play along the Cherry Lane.
Without his lifelong friend, Puff could not be brave
So, Puff that mighty dragon sadly slipped into his cave, oh

Chorus:

— SOME FAMOUS CONCERT HALLS —

Name	Country	Founded/Built
Royal Albert Hall	UK	1871
Concertgebouw	Netherlands	1888
Boston Symphony Hall	USA	1900
Beijing Concert Hall	China	1985
National Concert Hall	Ireland	1981
Royal Festival Hall	UK	1951
Tchaikovsky Concert Hall	Russia	1940
Perth Concert Hall	Australia	1973
Carnegie Hall	USA	1891
The Rudolfinum	Czech Republic	1876–84

— THE ORCHESTRA PLAN —

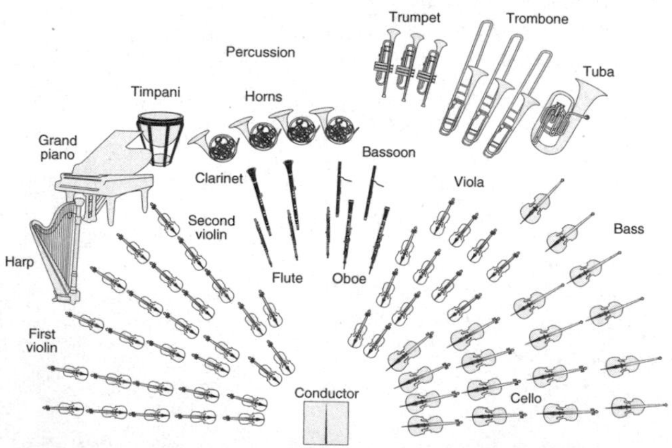

— 10 BARBERSHOP QUARTETS NOW OR ONCE — REGISTERED WITH THE SPEBSQSA

The SPEBSQSA is the Society for the Preservation and Encouragement of Barbershop Quartet Singing in America.

2 Boyz 2 Men
A Cafellas
The Achey-Breaky Parts
In Serious Treble
Internationally Renowned Mavulous Fabricks
Dispensers Of Musical Libations
Larry And Jerry Wit A Pair Of Genes
Four Get Me Notes
Rabinowitz, Rabinowitz, Rabinowitz And Raoul
Small, Medium, Large And Oh My Gosh

— HIP-HOP DICTIONARY —

All that – to possess positive qualities.
Battle – a competition between rappers, breakdancers or graffiti artists.
Beef – an argument between individuals or gangs.
Bite – to imitate someone else's style
Bling-bling – jewellery
Blunted – stoned, intoxicated on marajuana
Bounce – to leave, exit
Cheese – cash, wealth.
Chickenhead – an idiot
Chill – to relax.
Chronic – disturbingly potent marijuana or weed laced with cocaine.
Crib – home.
Fly – attractive
Fresh – new, excellent
Ill – obnoxious or arrogant
Phat – very good, very well done
Serve up – to beat an opponent in a competition
Wack – rubbish, crazy or weird.

— TEN CLASSICS WRITTEN BY CAROLE KING —

The Shirelles	'Will You Love Me Tomorrow'	Scepter	1961
Bobby Vee	'Take Good Care Of My Baby'	Liberty	1961
Donny Osmond	'Go Away Little Girl'	MGM	1971
Little Eva	'The Locomotion'	Dimension	1972
James Taylor	'You've Got A Friend'	Warner	1971
The Animals	'Don't Bring Me Down'	MGM	1966
Aretha Franklin	'You Make Me Feel Like A Natural Woman'	Atlantic	1967
The Monkees	'Pleasant Valley Sunday'	Colgems	1967
Herman's Hermits	'I'm Into Something Good'	MGM	1964
The Drifters	'Up On The Roof'	Atlantic	1963

— YODELLING —

Yodelling was originally known as *juchizn* before it became an art form and expanded into the Swiss and Bavarian Alps. Most of the words in yodeling don't mean anything – they are chosen for their sounds. Sometimes, though, a yodel piece ends with three or four meaningful words, just for the fun of it. Yodels were largely an oral tradition until the likes of Tobi Reiser, a folk-music pioneer, began writing the melodies down. The style was employed by many black singers in the 19th century and reached a peak in the 1920s via the songs of country singer Jimmie Rodgers. It has also been employed in jazz music by the likes of Louis Armstrong and in jazz-funk music by the likes of Leon Thomas.

— FAMOUS CONSERVATORIES —

Name	Country	Founded/Built
Moscow Conservatory	Russia	1866
St Petersburg Conservatory	Russia	1862
Paris Conservatory	France	1795
Juilliard	USA	1905
Leipzig	Germany	1843
National Conservatory Of Music	USA	1885
Santa Maria de Lorento	Naples	1537
Oberlin Conservatory Of Music	USA	1865
Prague Conservatory	Czech Republic	1808
Brussels Conservatory	Belgium	1813

— TEN CLASSICS PRODUCED BY PHIL SPECTOR —

The Teddy Bears	'To Know Him Is To Love Him'	Dore	1958
Righteous Brothers	'You've Lost That Loving Feeling'	Philles	1965
The Ronettes	'Be My Baby'	Philles	1963
George Harrison	'My Sweet Lord'	Apple	1970
Righteous Brothers	'Unchained Melody'	Philles	1970
The Crystals	'Da Doo Ron Ron'	Philles	1963
Bob B Soxx And The Blue Jeans	'Zip-A-Dee Doo Dah'	Philles	1963
John Lennon/ Plastic Ono Band	'Imagine'	Apple	1971
Curtis Lee	'Pretty Little Angel Eyes'	Dunes	1961
The Crystals	'Then He Kissed Me'	Philles	1963

— DISCO RECORD —

The world's largest disco took place at the Buffalo Convention Center, New York, in 1979, with 13,000 people.

**In August 1983, Peter Stewart of Birmingham, England, set a world record by disco dancing for 408 hours.*

— EMBOUCHURES —

The manner in which the lips and tongue are applied to a musical mouthpiece is called an *embouchure*. Most embouchures are named after musicians:

The Farkas embouchure,
The Stevens/Costello embouchure,
The Superchops or Callet embochure,
The Maggio embouchure

— MEMBERS OF THE NATIVE TONGUE MOVEMENT —

De La Soul
The Jungle Brothers
Queen Latifah
A Tribe Called Quest
Black Sheep
Monie Love

— LARGEST CONCERT AUDIENCE FOR A ROCK ARTIST —

The largest paying audience ever attracted by a solo performer was an estimated 180,000–184,000, in the Maracanã Stadium, Rio de Janeiro, Brazil, at a Paul McCartney concert held on 21 April 1990.

**The largest free rock-concert attendance was Rod Stewart's free concert at Copacabana Beach, Rio de Janeiro, Brazil, on New Year's Eve, 1994. It reportedly attracted an audience of 3.5 million.*

THE FIRST PERFORMER — TO SELL A MILLION RECORDS —

Enrico Caruso (1873-1921) was an Italian tenor whose career happily coincided with the rise of the gramophone. The Victor Talking Machine Company were at the time competing with Edison's National Phonograph Company. Victor knew they had to find something to compete with the Edison name, so they began marketing Caruso's voice as the perfect voice to listen to on their machine. The masses bought it and Caruso was able to sell a million copies of his *Vesti La Giubba* (from *I Pagliacci*).

— LOUIE LOUIE —

When The Kingsmen's song 'Louie Louie' was released in 1663, rumours began to fly that it contained obscene lyrics. The FBI began an investigation which lasted an incredible two years and managed to uncover very little information. The lengthy investigative process included repeated listenings of the song at different speeds and interviews with the songwriter, Richard Berry, members of The Kingsmen and others. The FBI eventually concluded that the song was unintelligible at any speed. Thanks at least partially to its notoriety, it is one of the most covered songs in history. In August 1983, KFJC Radio, a college radio station in Los Altos Hills, California, held an event called 'Maximum Louie Louie' where they played 823 versions of the song back to back. It took 63 hours and 14 minutes.

— AUM —

The AUM symbol is the most sacred symbol in Hindu dharma, symbolising the infinite Brahman (ultimate reality) and the entire universe. There are three sorts of repetitions of these mantras. One is the verbal, another semi-verbal, and the third mental. The repetition which is loud is the verbal; the next one is where only the lips move but no sound is heard. The inaudible repetition of the Mantra, accompanied with the thinking of its meaning, is called the 'mental repetition' and is the highest.

— TEN CLASSICS PENNED BY BURT BACHARACH —

Christopher Cross	'Arthur's Theme'	Warner Bros	1981
Perry Como	'Magic Moments'	RCA	1958
Dionne Warwick	'I Say A Little Prayer'	Scepter	1967
Dusty Springfield	'The Look Of Love'	Philips	1967
BJ Thomas	'Raindrops Keep Falling On My Head'	Scepter	1970
The Carpenters	'(They Long To Be) Close To You'	A&M	1970
Dionne Warwick	'Walk On By'	Scepter	1964
The Naked Eyes	'Always Something There To Remind Me'	EMI America	1983
Jerry Butler	'Make It Easy On Yourself'	Vee Jay	1962
The Drifters	'Please Stay'	Atlantic	1961

— JAMES BOND THEME TUNES —

The James Bond movies have produced more than 20 chart-topping hits from 20 movies over a 40-year run. The majority of the musical scores are credited to John Barry, who scored 12 of the 20. Other composers of the soundtracks have been David Arnold, George Martin, Marvin Hamlish, Bill Conti, Michael Kamen and Eric Serra.

James Bond Theme – Monty Norman Ochestra (from Dr. No) 1962
From Russia With Love – Matt Monro 1963
Goldfinger – Shirley Bassey 1964
Thunderball – Tom Jones 1965
007 – John Barry (from *Thunderball*) 1965
You Only Live Twice – Nancy Sinatra 1967
On Her Majesty's Secret Service – John Barry And His Orchestra 1969
Diamonds Are Forever – Shirley Bassey 1971
Live And Let Die – Wings 1973
Man With The Golden Gun – Lulu 1974
Nobody Does It Better – Carly Simon 1977
Moonraker –Shirley Bassey 1979
For Your Eyes Only – Sheena Easton (from *The Spy Who Loved Me*) 1981
All Time High – Rita Coolidge (from Octopussy) 1983
A View To A Kill – Duran Duran 1985
The Living Daylights – A-Ha 1987
Licensed To Kill – Gladys Knight 1989
Goldeneye – Tina Turner 1995
Tomorrow Never Dies – Sheryl Crow 1997
The World Is Not Enough – Garbage 1999
Die Another Day – Madonna 2002

— OLDEST JAZZ CLUB —

The Village Vanguard cellar jazz club opened in New York City, USA, in 1935 and has hosted mainstream jazz concerts ever since. Artists who have appeared there include John Coltrane, Miles Davis, Stan Getz, Wynton Marsalis and Thelonious Monk.

— THE MOST VALUABLE GUITAR IN THE WORLD —

Jerry Garcia's 'Tiger' guitar sold for $850,000 (£583,992) to an anonymous bidder at a Guernsey's auction in New York, USA, on 9 May 2002. At the same auction, another of Jerry Garcia's guitars, called 'Wolf', sold for $700,000 (£436,449). The buyer's commission pushed the price paid for 'Tiger' to $957,500 (£596,996) and for 'Wolf' to $789,500 (£497,860).

— DIFFERENT TYPES OF HARMONICA —

Double Reed
Classical
Diatonic
Chromatic
Tremolo
Octave Tuned
Special Tuned Diatonic
Bass
Chord
Polyphonias
Four-Hole

— THE BEST OF ENNIO MORRICONE —

Born in Rome in 1928, Ennio Morricone is one of the giants of film music. He has provided nearly 400 movie scores, and although he's never won an Oscar, he's been nominated for five. Indicative of his wide appeal is the fact that Metallica sometimes start their shows with Morricone's 'The Ecstasy In Gold' from the film *The Good, The Bad And The Ugly*.

The Untouchables 1987 (dir Brian De Palma)
Once Upon A Time In America 1984 (dir Sergio Leone)
Casualties Of War 1989 (dir Brian De Palma)
In The Line Of Fire 1993 (dir Wolfgang Petersen)
The Thing 1982 (dir John Carpenter)
The Good The Bad And The Ugly 1966 (dir Sergio Leone)
A Fistful Of Dollars 1964 (dir Sergio Leone)
For A Few Dollars More 1965 (dir Sergio Leone)
Once Upon A Time In The West 1968 (dir Sergio Leone)
Cinema Paradiso 1988 (dir Giuseppe Tornatore)
The Phantom Of The Opera 1998 (dir Dario Argento)
Lolita 1997 (dir Adrian Lyne)

— TEN SONGS BY HOLLAND DOZIER HOLLAND —

The Supremes	'Where Did Our Love Go'	Motown	1964
The Four Tops	'I Can't Help Myself (Sugar Pie Honey Punch)'	Motown	1965
The Supremes	'Stop In The Name Of Love'	Motown	1965
The Marvelettes	'Please Mr Postman'	Tamla	1961
The Four Tops	'Reach Out I'll Be There'	Motown	1966
Freda Payne	'Band Of Gold'	Invictus	1970
The Temptations	'Beauty Is Only Skin Deep'	Gordy	1966
Marvin Gaye	'How Sweet It Is To Be Loved By You'	Tamla	1965
The Chairmen Of The Board	'Give Me Just A Little More Time'	Invictus	1970
Marvin Gaye	'Can I Get A Witness'	Tamla	1963

— THE OLDEST CONTINUALLY PLAYED — COURT MUSIC IN THE WORLD

Gagaku (translation: elegant music) has been played at the Japaense imperial court for over 1200 years. It can be categorised into three different parts: instrumental music and dance deriving from the Asian mainland; accompanied vocal music and dance for shinto rituals; accompanied vocal music originating at the Japanese court of the ninth to the twelfth century.

THE SACHS-HORNBOSTEL — SYSTEM OF INSTRUMENT CLASSIFICATION (1914) —

In 1914, Erich Moritz Von Hornbostel and Curt Sachs categorised musical instruments into family groupings based on the nature of the initial vibrating body. Their system is based on one devised in the late 19th century by Victor Mahillon, the curator of Brussels Conservatory's musical instrument collection, and allows any instrument from any culture to be classified within it.

Idiophones – Instruments that are struck, shaken, plucked or rubbed, such as bells, cymbals, rattles, claves, marimbas and harmonicas.

Membranophones – Instruments that produce sound by means of a stretched skin, or membrane, such as kettledrums, snare drums and tambourines.

Aerophones – Instruments that make sound with vibrating air, such as trumpets, horns, clarinets, saxaphones, didgeridoos and flutes.

Chordophones – Instruments that use strings, such as pianos, guitars, zithers, lutes, lyres and harps.

Electrophones – Instruments using electronic circuits or amplification of sound, such as electric guitars or electric pianos.

TEN CLASSICS PENNED BY — KENNY GAMBLE AND LEON HUFF —

MFSB	'TSOP' (The Sound Of Philadelphia)	PIR	1974
Thelma Houston	'Don't Leave Me This Way'	Tamla	1977
The O'Jays	'Love Train'	PIR	1973
Harold Melvin And The Blue Notes	'If You Don't Know Me By Now'	PIR	1972
Heavy D And The Boyz	'Now That We Found Love'	Uptown	1991
The O'Jays	'For The Love Of Money'	PIR	1974
Billy Paul	'Me And Mrs Jones'	PIR	1972
Lou Rawls	'You'll Never Find Another Love Like Mine'	PIR	1976
The Three Degrees	'When Will I See You Again'	PIR	1974
The Jacksons	'Enjoy Yourself'	Epic	1977

— THE KHAEN —

The *khaen* (pronounced 'cane') is a mouth organ fashioned from bamboo and wood and found throughout Eastern Asia. It is one of the oldest harmonic instruments in the world. Its most important function for the Hmong people is during funeral ceremonies, when it is played continuously for many days. The soul of the deceased cannot return to the ancestors without this ceremony, which is fundamental to the Hmong world view.

SOME INTERESTING ELECTRONIC — INSTRUMENTS AND THEIR INVENTORS —

Instrument	Inventor	Country	Date
Musical Telegraph	Elisha Grey	USA	1876
Telharmonium	Thaddeus Cahill	USA	1897
Intonarumori	Luigi Russolo	Italy	1913
Theremin	Leon Theremin	Soviet Union	1917
Ondes-Martenot	Maurice Martenot	France	1928
Hellertion	B Helberger and P Lertes	Germany	1929
Trautonium	Dr Freidrich Trautwein	Germany	1930
Trillion Tone Organ	A Lesti and F Sammis	USA	1931
Variophone	Yevgeny Sholpo	Soviet Union	1932
Hammond Organ	Laurens Hammond	USA	1935
Heliophon	Bruno Hellberger	Germany	1936
Singing Keyboard	F Sammis	USA	1936
Univox	Univox Co	UK	1940
Electronic Sackbut	Hugh Le Caine	Canada	1945
Clavioline	M Constant Martin	France	1947
Melochord	Harald Bode	Germany	1947
Dr Kent's Electronic Music Box	Dr Earle Kent	USA	1951
Clavivox	Raymond Scott	USA	1952
Composertron	Osmond Kendall	Canada	1953
Music I-V Software	Max Mathews	USA	1957
Moog Synthesiser	Robert Moog	USA	1963
Mellotron	Leslie Bradley	UK	1963
Buchla Synthesiser	Donald Buchla	USA	1963
Arp Synthesiser	Philip Dodds	USA	1964
Electronium-Scott	Raymond Scott	USA	1970
Maplin Synthesiser	Trevor G Marshall	Australia/USA	1973
Synclavier	New England Digital Corporation	USA	1975
Korg Synthesiser	Korg	Japan	1975
Oberheim Synthesiser	Thomas Oberheim	USA	1978
Fairlight CMI	Peter Vogel and Kim Ryrie	Australia	1979
Emulator	Emu Systems	USA	1981

— ALEATORY MUSIC —

Aleatory is the term applied to an extremely random style of music where the composer and/or the performer randomly picks musical materials to create a piece of music. It is a latter-day version of 18th-century 'dice music', in which dice were used to determine which measures of the composition would be played. In aleatory music, the composer does not specify particular pitches, rhythms or tone colours, but gives ranges of these materials and relies on chance procedures/performers to select and shape them. There are no rules – any kind of music can be created as a result. Aleatoric composers include John Cage, Earle Brown, Morton Feldman, Christian Wolff, Pierre Boulez and Karlheinz Stockhausen.

— VOLUME DYNAMICS —

Dynamic	Notation	Meaning
Piano-pianissimo	*ppp*	As soft as possible
Pianissimo	*pp*	Very soft
Piano	*p*	Soft
Mezzo piano	*mp*	Moderately soft
Mezzo forte	*mf*	Moderately loud
Forte	*f*	Loud
Fortissimo	*ff*	Very loud
Forte-fortissimo	*fff*	As loud as possible
Sforzando, sforzato	*sf*, *sfz*	Forcing, accented
Rinforzando	*rfz*	Reinforcing
Forte piano	*fp*	Loud, then soft
Forzando	*fz*	Forcing, a sudden accent
Crescendo	*Cresc*	Gradually sing louder
Decrescendo	*Decresc*	Gradually sing softer
Diminuendo	*Dim*	Becoming gradually softer

TEN CLASSICS PRODUCED — BY STOCK, AITKEN AND WATERMAN —

Rick Astley	'Never Gonna Give You Up'	RCA	1988
Bananarama	'Venus'	London	1986
Kylie Minogue	'The Locomotion'	Geffen	1980
Dead Or Alive	'You Spin Me Round (Like A Record)'	Epic	1985
Rick Astley	'Together Forever'	RCA	1988
Nicki French	'Total Eclipse Of The Heart'	Critique	1995
Boy Krazy	'That's What Love Can Do'	Next Plateau	1993
Bananarama	'I Heard A Rumour'	London	1987
Donna Summer	'This Time I Know It's For Real'	Atlantic	1989
Rick Astley	'It Would Take A Strong Man'	RCA	1988

— VOICE CLASSIFICATIONS —

Soprano Highest female voice.

Mezzo-soprano/mezzo Middle female voice.

Contralto/alto Lowest female voice.

Tenor Highest male voice (in most operas).

Baritone Middle male voice.

Bass Lowest male voice.

Bass-baritone Rare male voice.

Coloratura Unusually flexible voice

Dramatic Heaviest voice

Falsetto The upper part of a voice in which the vocal cords do not vibrate completely

Helden A large voice

Lyric Light- to medium-weight voice

Soubrette A soprano or mezzo-soprano

Spinto Medium to heavy voice

— BRIAN ENO'S FULL NAME —

Brian Peter St John Le Baptiste De La Salle Eno

— A COLLECTION OF USEFUL — ELECTRONIC INITIALS

ADC: Analogue-to-Digital Converter
ADSR: Attack/Decay/Sustain/Release
AIFF: Audio Interchange File Format
BPM: Beats Per Minute
CD-ROM: Compact Disc Read-Only Memory
dB: Decibel
DSP: Digital Signal Processing
FFT: Fast Fourier Transform
FM: Frequency Modulation
GM: General MIDI
Hz: Hertz
IRQ: Interrupt Request Level
LFO: Low-Frequency Oscillator
MCI: Media Control Interface
MIDI: Musical Instrument Digital Interface
MTC: MIDI Time Code
OMS: Open Music System
PCM: Pulse Code Modulation
RAM: Random Access Memory
ROM: Read-Only Memory
SCSI: Small Computer Systems Interface (pronounced 'scuzzy')
SDS: MIDI Sample Dump Standard
SND: Sound Resource
SPP: Song Position Pointer
THD: Total Harmonic Distortion
VCA: Voltage-Controlled Amplifier
VCF: Voltage-Controlled Filter
VCO: Voltage-Controlled Oscillator
.WAV: the Windows audio file format

— THE SMALLEST MUSICAL INSTRUMENT — IN THE WORLD

The Nanoharp, an instrument developed by researchers in Nanotechnology at Cornwell University, is carved out of a single crystal of silicon and is about the size of a red blood cell. The strings are silicon rods 50 nanometres (nm – one billionth of a meter) in diameter and range from about 1,000–8,000nm long. Each string is about 150 atoms thick and vibrate at frequencies as high as 380MHz. This frequency is inaudible to the human ear (the human ear cannot hear frequencies above 22KHz), and is too high even for dogs. Cornell University scientists hope to use it to study the properties of extremely tiny vibrating systems.

— SOME IMPORTANT RULES FOR THE OULO — AIR GUITAR WORLD CHAMPIONSHIPS

- Air guitarists' guitars must be invisible, ie made from air.
- Air guitarists can play electric or acoustic air guitar, or both.
- Help from personal air roadies is allowed. Duets or backing bands – air or real – are not allowed.
- Air guitarists' performance must be a solo performance.
- Props like plectrums and costumes can be used in a preferred way.
- Contestants take part in the competition at their own risk.

— UK NORTHERN SOUL CLUBS —

During the 1970s, Wigan Casino and Blackpool Mecca were two focal points for the all-night dancing to '60s and '70s American soul classics known as northern soul. Much of the music that was played in the clubs of northern England during this period was relatively obscure in the USA, even though it was produced there.

The Golden Torch	Wigan Casino
The Catacombs	Top Of The World
Blackpool Mecca	The Twisted Wheel
Va Va's	

— MEMBERS OF THE CHICAGO BLUES SCHOOL —

Buddy Guy
Lonnie Brooks
James Cotton
Jimmy Reed
Son Seals
Hound Dog Taylor
Muddy Waters
Ronnie Baker Brooks
Arthur Crudup
Earl Hooker
Otis Rush
Magic Slim
Koko Taylor
Junior Wells
Paul Butterfield
Willie Dixon
Elmore James
Magic Sam
Otis Spann
Little Walter
Howlin' Wolf

— SOME FEMALE BLUES SINGERS —

Lucille Bogan (1897-1948)
Ida Cox (1896-1967)
Ma Rainey (1886-1939)
Bessie Smith (d 1937)
Lucille Hegamin (d 1970)
Mamie Smith (1883-1946)
Trixie Smith (1895-1943)
Victoria Spivey (d 1976)
Sippie Wallace (1898-1986)
Willie Mae Thornton (1926-1984)
Etta James (b 1938)
Gladys Bentley (1907-1960)
Ethel Waters (1896-1977)
Alberta Hunter (1895-1984)
Bonnie Raitt (b 1949)

— THE MOST RECORDED SONG IN THE WORLD —

At the last count there were over 1,600 versions of 'Yesterday' by Paul McCartney and John Lennon. The song, covered by everyone from Elvis Presley, Boyz II Men, Frank Sinatra, James Brown and Gladys Knight, famously came to McCartney in a dream. He woke up, went to the piano, turned on the tape recorder, and played the song, using the words 'scrambled eggs' initially to remember the tune. He wisely replaced them with 'yesterday' later on.

— CURIOUSLY NAMED POP-STAR OFFSPRING —

Keith Richards
Dandelion & Marlon & Alexandra Nicole & Theodora Dupree

David Bowie
Zowie

Posh Spice
Brooklyn & Romeo

Smokey Robinson
Tamla & Berry

Bob Geldof
Fifi Trixibelle & Peaches & Pixie

Michael Hutchence
Heavenly Hiraani Tigerlily

Buffy Sainte-Marie
Dakota Star Blanket Wolfchild

Frank Zappa
Dweezil & Moon Unit & Ahmet Emuuka Rodin & Diva

Marc Bolan
Rolan

Aretha Franklin
Kecalf

Billy Swan
Planet & Sierra

Donovan
Oriole & Julian & Astrella & Donovan Jr & Ione

Eric Burdon
Mirage

Bono
Elijah Bob Patricius Guggi Q & Memphis Eve & Jordan & John

Sonny And Cher
Chastity

Dave Stewart
Django & Sam Hurricane

Scary Spice
Phoenix Chi

Madonna
Lourdes & Rocco

Noel Gallagher
Anais

— THE MEMORABLE WHISTLING LINE MIXTAPE — (MUSIC TO WASH UP TO)

Ennio Morricone – 'The Good, The Bad And The Ugly'
Rolling Stones – 'Walking The Dog'
Bangles – 'Walk Like An Egyptian'
David Bowie – 'Golden Years'
De La Soul – 'Eye Know'
Peter Gabriel – 'Games Without Frontiers'
Monty Python – 'Always Look On The Bright Side Of Life'
Guns N' Roses – 'Patience'
John Lennon – 'Jealous Guy'
Otis Redding – 'Sittin' On The Dock Of The Bay'
The Pixies – 'La La Love You'
The Small Faces – 'Lazy Sunday'
Frenzal Rhomb – 'Summer's Here'
The Beatles – 'Two Of Us'
Paper Lace – 'Billy Don't Be A Hero'
Paul Simon – 'Me And Julio Down By The Schoolyard'
The Scorpions – 'Wind Of Change'
Bobby McFerrin – 'Don't Worry, Be Happy'

— MARIAN AT THE METROPOLITAN —

Marian Anderson was the first black soloist to sing at the Metropolitan Opera House, New York City, in 1955.

— THE FASTEST PLAYING OF THE SAILOR'S HORNPIPE —

Trombonist Peter 'Fats' Baxter of Hove, England, played the old English folk tune 'The Sailor's Hornpipe' in 8.5 seconds at the House of Commons, Westminster, London, England, on 15 December 1998.

— ON MUSIC —

'Information is not knowledge. Knowledge is not wisdom. Wisdom is not truth. Truth is not beauty. Beauty is not love. Love is not music. Music is the best.' *Frank Zappa*

'Music is spiritual. The music business is not.' *Van Morrison*

'Music should strike fire from the heart of man, and bring tears from the eyes of woman.' *Ludwig van Beethoven*

'Music is the art of sounds in the movement of time.' *Ferruccio Busoni*

'It is cruel, you know, that music should be so beautiful. It has the beauty of loneliness and of pain, of strength and freedom. The beauty of disappointment and never-satisfied love. The cruel beauty of nature, and everlasting beauty of monotony.' *Benjamin Britten*

'Music is well said to be the speech of angels; in fact, nothing among the utterances allowed to man is felt to be so divine. It brings us near to the infinite.' *Thomas Carlyle*

'Without music, life is a journey through a desert.' *Pat Conroy*

'Music is the vernacular of the human soul.' *Geoffrey Latham*

'Music is a beautiful opiate, if you don't take it too seriously.' *Henry Miller*

'Music is the key to the female heart.' *Johann G Seume*

'Music is essentially useless, as life is.' *George Santayana*

'Music washes away from the soul the dust of everyday life.' *Red Auerbach*

'Music is the only noise for which one is obliged to pay.' *Alexandre Dumas*

'Music is life, and, like it, inextinguishable.' *Carl Nielsen*

'Music is the most disagreeable and the most widely beloved of all noises.' *T Gautier*

'All music's folk music – leastways, I never heard of no horse making it.' *Louis Armstrong and Big Bill Broonzy*

'Much music marreth men's manners.' *Galen*

'Music is no different than opium. Music affects the human mind in a way that makes people think of nothing but music and sensual matters... Music is a treason to the country, a treason to our youth, and we should cut out all this music and replace it with something more instructive.' *Ayatollah Khomeini*

'Music should be a collective magic and hysteria.' *Pierre Boulez*

'After silence, that which comes nearest to expressing the inexpressible is music.' *Aldous Huxley*

'One good thing about music, when it hits you, you feel no pain.' *Bob Marley*

'Music is the silence between the notes.' *Claude Debussy*

'Without music to decorate it, time is just a bunch of boring production deadlines or dates by which bills must be paid.' *Frank Zappa*

'The music business is a cruel and shallow trench, a long plastic hallway where thieves and pimps run free, and good men lie like dogs. There is also a negative side.' *Hunter S Thompson*

'Music is the wine that fills the cup of silence.' *Robert Fripp*

'The public doesn't want new music; the main thing it demands of a composer is that he be dead.' *Arthur Honegger*

— ON MUSIC (CONTINUED) —

'All the sounds on the Earth are like music.' *Oscar Hammerstein II*

'Sugar is not so sweet to the palate as sound to the healthy ear.' *Ralph Waldo Emerson*

'If music be the food of love, play on: give me excess of it...' *William Shakespeare*

'Music is given to us with the sole purpose of establishing an order in things, including, and particularly, the co-ordination between man and time.' *Igor Stravinsky*

'The whole problem can be stated quite simply by asking, "Is there a meaning to music?" My answer would be, "Yes." And "Can you state in so many words what the meaning is?", my answer to that would be, "No."' *Aaron Copland*

'Music is everybody's possession. Only publishers think that people own it.' *John Lennon*

'Music melts all the separate parts of our bodies together.' *Anais Nin*

— WINNERS OF THE EUROVISION SONG CONTEST —

2002	Latvia	Marie N	'I Wanna'
2001	Estonia	Tanel Padar, Dave Benton And 2xl	'Everybody'
2000	Denmark	Olsen Brothers	'Fly On The Wings Of Love'
1999	Sweden	Charlotte Nilsson	'Take Me To Your Heaven'
1998	Israel	Dana International	'Diva'
1997	UK	Katrina And The Waves	'Love Shine A Light'
1996	Ireland	Eimear Quinn	'The Voice'
1995	Norway	Secret Garden	'Nocturne'
1994	Ireland	Paul Harrington And Charlie McGettigan	'Rock 'n' Roll Kids'
1993	Ireland	Niamh Kavanagh	'In Your Eyes'
1992	Ireland	Linda Martin	'Why Me?'
1991	Sweden	Carola	'Fångad Av En Stormvind'

1990	Italy	Toto Cutugno	'Insieme: 1992'
1989	Yugoslavia	Riva	'Rock Me'
1988	Switzerland	Celine Dion	'Ne Partez Pas Sans Moi'
1987	Ireland	Johnny Logan	'Hold Me Now'
1986	Belgium	Sandra Kim	'J'aime La Vie'
1985	Norway	Bobbysocks	'La Det Swinge'
1984	Sweden	The Herreys	'Diggi-Loo Diggi-Ley'
1983	Luxembourg	Corinne Hermes	'Si La Vie Est Cadeau'
1982	Germany	Nicole	'Ein Bisschen Frieden'
1981	UK	Bucks Fizz	'Making Your Mind Up'
1980	Ireland	Johnny Logan	'What's Another Year?'
1979	Israel	Gali Atari & Milk And Honey	'Hallelujah'
1978	Israel	Izhar Cohen & Alphabeta	'A-Ba-Ni-Bi'
1977	France	Marie Myriam	'L'oiseau Et L'enfant'
1976	UK	Brotherhood Of Man	'Save Your Kisses For Me'
1975	Netherlands	Teach-In	'Ding-A-Dong'
1974	Sweden	Abba	'Waterloo'
1973	Luxembourg	Anne-Marie David	'Tu Te Reconnaitras'
1972	Luxembourg	Vicky Leandros	'Après Toi'
1971	Monaco	Severine	'Un Banc, Un Arbre, Une Rue'
1970	Ireland	Dana	'All Kinds Of Everything'
1969	Spain	Salome	'Vivo Cantando'
1969	Netherlands	Lenny Kuhr	'De Troubadour'
1969	UK	Lulu	'Boom-Bang-A-Bang'
1969	France	Frida Boccara	'Un Jour, Un Enfant'
1968	Spain	Massiel	'La, La, La'
1967	UK	Sandie Shaw	'Puppet On A String'
1966	Austria	Udo Jürgens	'Mercie, Chérie'
1965	Luxembourg	France Gall	'Poupée De Cire, Poupée De Son'
1964	Italy	Gigliola Cinquetti	'Non Ho L'eta'
1963	Denmark	Grethe And Jørgen Ingmann	'Dansevise'
1962	France	Isabelle Aubret	'Un Premier Amour'
1961	Luxembourg	Jean-Claude Pascal	'Nous Les Amoureux'
1960	France	Jacqueline Boyer	'Tom Pillibi'
1959	Netherlands	Teddy Scholten	'Een Beetje'
1958	France	Andre Claveau	'Dors, Mon Amour'
1957	Netherlands	Corrie Brokken	'Net Als Toen'
1956	Switzerland	Lys Assia	'Refrain'

— MIDI —

Musical Instruments Digital Interface, a standard digital 'language' invented by American company Sequential Circuits in the early 1980s allowing musical instruments and related devices from any manufacturer to communicate with one another via a simple cable.

— GING GANG GOOLIE —

Ging gang goolie goolie goolie goolie whatcha,
Ging gang goo, ging gang goo,
Ging gang goolie goolie goolie goolie whatcha,
Ging gang goo, ging gang goo.

Hey-lah, hey-lah, shey-lah,
Hey-lah, shey-lah, hey-lah,
Ho – oh,
Hey-lah, hey-lah, shey-lah,
Hey-lah, shey-lah, hey-lah, ho.

Shilla-willa, shilla-willa,
Shilla-willa, shilla-willa,
Oompah, oompah,
Oompah, oompah...

— NIPPER THE HMV DOG —

Nipper, the famous dog associated with His Masters Voice, was real. He lived in Bristol, England with his owner, Mark Barraud. When Barraud died, the dog was adopted by his brother Francis, a painter, who made the famous portrait of Nipper looking puzzled at the voices he heard coming out of a phonograph. Francis contacted the Edison Bell Cylinder Phonograph Company to try to sell them the painting. They turned his offer down, so he visited the Gramophone Company instead, who said that, if he changed the phonograph to a gramophone, they would purchase it. Barraud had named the painting 'His Master's Voice', and this was first used as a slogan in 1907. The painting and its title were registered as trademarks in 1910. Today the image is used by EMI as the marketing identity for their HMV shops in the UK and Europe.

— BACKMASKING —

The process of encoding backwards messages in songs – backmasking – was pioneered most famously by The Beatles, who intentionally put hidden messages in some of their records. Some backmasks, however, are unintentional and have been 'discovered' after recording. The classic example of the unintentional backmask is Led Zepellin's 'Stairway To Heaven', which according to rock lore possesses no fewer than seven Satan-referencing messages in less than a minute. The band claim they knew nothing about these message while recording.

Artist	Song	Backmasked Message
The Beatles	'Rain'	'When the rain comes they run and hide their heads.'
Frank Zappa	'Ya Hozna'	'Yeah, right. Faster, faster. Go. Do it, do it. Right. Yeah. I'm feeling good. I'm looking great. Yeah, for sure. Like, no way'
Madonna	'Like A Prayer'	'Hear our saviour Satan.'
Pink Floyd	'Empty Spaces'	'Congratulations, you have just found the secret message. Please send your answer to Old Pink, care of the Funny Farm.'
Prince	'Darling Nikki'	'Hello. How are you? I'm fine 'cos I know that the Lord is coming soon. Coming, coming soon.'
Electric Light Orchestra	'Free On High'	'The music is reversible, but time – turn back! Turn back! Turn back! Turn back!'
The Eagles	'Hotel California'	'Yes, Satan had help. He organized his own religion. How nice it was – delicious. He puts it in a vat and fixes for his son and gives it away.'
Michael Jackson	'Beat It'	'I do believe it was Satan – in me.'

— BACKMASKING (CONTINUED) —

U2	'With Or Without You'	'We slap you too; we slap you. Hey, why not?'
Metallica	'Am I Evil?'	'Oh-oh, I am Satan, I am, I am. Oh, yeah I'm it. Yeah, I'm Satan, Oh yeah I'm it. Yes, I'm it.'
Led Zeppelin	'Stairway To Heaven'	'Cos I live with Satan' / 'The piper's calling you' / 'The lord turns me off' / 'There is power in Satan' / 'He will give you, give you 666' / 'I gotta live for Satan'

— NICKNAMES —

Frank Sinatra – 'Ol' Blue Eyes'
The Stranglers – 'The Meninblack'
Johnny Cash – 'The Man In Black'
Otis Redding – 'The Bear'
Grandmaster Flash – 'Toscaninni Of The Turntables'
Edith Piaf – 'Kid Sparrow'
Billie Holiday – 'Lady Day'
Gene Pitney – 'The Rockville Rocket'
Eric Clapton – 'Slowhand'
Charlie Parker – 'Bird'
Roy Orbison – 'The Big O'
Shirly Bassey – 'Burly Chassis'
Jerry Garcia – 'Captain Trips'
Jerry Lee Lewis – 'The Killer'
The Beatles – 'The Fab Four'
David Bowie – 'The Thin White Duke'
Tom Jones – 'The Twisting Vocalist From Pontypridd'
Louis Armstrong – 'Satchmo'
Michael Jackson – 'Wacko Jacko'
Madonna – 'Madge'
Babe Ruth – 'The Bambino'
Milt Jackson – 'Bags'
Barry White – 'Walrus Of Love'
Jimmie Rodgers – 'The Singing Brakeman'
Marilyn Manson – 'The God Of Fuck'

— THE LONGEST ALBUM TITLE —

When The Pawn Hits The Conflicts He Thinks Like A King What He Knows Throws The Blows When He Goes To The Fight And He'll Win The Whole Thing 'Fore He Enters The Ring There's No Body To Batter When Your Mind Is Your Might So When You Go Solo, You Hold Your Own Hand And Remember That Depth Is The Greatest Of Heights And If You Know Where You Stand, Then You Know Where To Land And If You Fall It Won't Matter, Cuz You'll Know That You're Right.

By Fiona Apple, released on Sony/Epic 1999.

— HOW TO PLAY THE TRIANGLE (STEP BY STEP) —

- Place the triangle in your non-dominant hand.
- Hold clip betwixt thumb and third finger.
- Place index finger above clip.
- Position open end of triangle close to the hand holding it.
- Hold the triangle at eye level.
- Strike the triangle on the bottom cross bar, either near the closed corner or on the closed side near the top.
- Use the natural weight of the beater to strike the triangle naturally.
- Use the fingers and wrist when using the beater – not the whole arm.
- Moving the triangle will create the Doppler effect.

— PHIL SPECTOR'S WALL OF SOUND —

The term 'wall of sound' was coined by the eccentric and legendary producer Phil Spector to describe the 'giant' sound he created by recording as many instruments as possible. One of the most in-demand rock and pop producers of the '60s, Spector often doubled or tripled up the same instruments, playing them as loudly as possible and liberally adding effects like reverb to give the impression that songs were recorded in a cathedral. His material is appositely described as 'little symphonies for the kiddies'.

— ELECTROMAGNETIC WAVELENGTHS —

Bandwidth Description	Frequency Range
Extremely Low Frequency (ELF)	0–3KHz
Very Low Frequency (VLF)	3–30KHz
Radio Navigation and Maritime Mobile	9–540KHz
Low Frequency (LF)	30–300KHz
Medium Frequency (MF)	300–3000KHz
AM Radio Broadcast	540–1630KHz
Travellers' Information Service	1610KHz
High Frequency (HF)	3–30MHz
Shortwave Broadcast Radio	5.95–26.1MHz
Very High Frequency (VHF)	30–300MHz
Low Band: TV Band 1 Channels 2–6	54–88MHz
Mid Band: FM Radio Broadcast	88–174 MHz
High Band: TV Band 2 – Channels 7-13	174–216MHz
Super Band (Mobile/Fixed Radio and TV)	216–600MHz
Ultra-High Frequency (UHF)	300–3,000MHz
Channels 14–70	470–806 MHz
L-Band:	500–1500 MHz
Personal Communications Services (PCS)	1850–1990 MHz
Unlicensed Pcs Devices	1910–1930 MHz
Superhigh Frequencies (SHF) (Microwave)	3–30GHz
C-Band	3.6–7.025GHz
X-Band:	7.25–8.4GHz
Ku-Band	10.7–14.5GHz
Ka-Band	17.3–31.0GHz
Extremely High Frequencies (EHF) (Millimeter Wave Signals)	30.0–300GHz
Additional Fixed Satellite	38.6–275GHz
Infrared Radiation	300–430THz
Visible Light	430–750 THz
Ultraviolet Radiation	1.62–30PHz
X-Rays	30PHz–30EHz
Gamma Rays	30–3,000 EHz

— BATONS AND BULLETS —

Artur Rodzinski conducted the New York Philharmonic in the 1940s with a loaded gun in his back pocket.

— SILBO —

Several communities around the world communicate via whistling. Perhaps the most well known are the inhabitants of La Gomera in the Canary Islands. Their language, known as Silbo, originated as a way for people to communicate across long distances, and has evolved into a method of communication that encodes sequences of Spanish phonemes into a signal. At a basic level, the language consists of two vowels and four consonants, with whistles of different tones or duration denoting each letter. An inhabitant of La Gomera set the world record for the farthest distance a human voice can travel – 17km (10.5 miles) across still water at night.

— TEN THINGS YOU POSSIBLY DIDN'T KNOW — ABOUT...ELVIS PRESLEY

- There are an estimated 35,000 Elvis impersonators, including a parachuting group called The Flying Elvises, who book themselves out to drop in on parties.
- Artist Maurice Bennett of New Zealand has made a portrait of Elvis from toast, cooked to varying shades of 'doneness' to achieve the correct shading and tones.
- Elvis's shoe size was 11D.
- Elvis once jumped on stage during a Tom Jones concert and gave a ten-minute karate demonstration.
- Elvis only ever played one encore – at a comeback gig in Hawaii.
- Elvis failed his music class in school.
- Elvis's underpants are worth an estimated $1,300 (£800).
- 7% of Americans think Elvis is alive.
- Elvis conversed with his mother in a strange baby talk that only they could understand
- By the time he was 40, Elvis's hair was totally white because he had abused it with dyes and products.

— THE INSIDE STORY OF PIANO WIRE —

Size	Diameter (")	Feet per lb (approx)
12	.029	445
12.5	.030	415
13	.031	384
13.5	.032	366
14	.033	330
14.5	.034	300
15	.035	295
15.5	.036	290
16	.037	275
16.5	.038	260
17	.039	248
17.5	.040	234
18	.041	223
18.5	.042	212
19	.043	200
19.5	.044	190
20	.045	182
20.5	.046	174
21	.047	165
21.5	.048	160
22	.049	156
23	.051	140
24	.055	125
25	.059	100

— A YODELLING CLASSIC —

'She Taught Me To Yodel'

I went across to Switzerland, where all the yodellers be,
To try to learn to yodel and go yodel-ay-hee-dee,
I climbed a big high mountain on a clear and sunny day,
And there I met a young Swiss girl up in a Swiss chalet.

She taught me how to yodel – (yodel)
She taught me how to yodel – (yodel)

This girl up in the mountains was a sweet lovely Swiss,
She taught me how to yodel and she taught me how to kiss,
She taught me how to cuddle in that good old mountain style,
We did our loving on an alp, and yodeled all the while.

This is how to yodel – (yodel)
This is how to yodel – (yodel)

And now I'm going to teach you all to yodel just like me,
It's easy while you're shining to go yodel-ay-hee-dee,
First you take a deep breath, then you exhale one, two, three,
And then you'll hear a yodel if you'll listen close to me.

This is how to yodel – (yodel)
This is how to yodel – (yodel)

— POPPED STARS (MURDERED MUSICIANS) —

Robert Johnson – poisoned with strychnine-laced whiskey – 1938

John Lennon – shot by crazed fan – 1980

Marvin Gaye – shot by his father following an argument – 1984

Peter Tosh – shot by burglars in his home – 1987

Little Walter – killed in a Chicago street fight – 1968

King Curtis – stabbed outside his New York City apartment – 1971

Sal Mineo – stabbed by a stranger in Los Angeles – 1976

John Lee 'Sonny Boy' Williamson – stabbed in the head outside his Chicago home – 1948

James Sheppard – shot on the Long Island Expressway – 1970

Samuel George – stabbed during an argument – 1982

Sam Cooke – shot after attacking a hotel manageress – 1964

Arthur 'T-Roy' Ross – murdered by suffocation – 1996

— THE FOUR FUNDAMENTAL ELEMENTS OF HIP-HOP —

Rapping • Breakdancing • Graffiti • DJing

— MOVIE HITS —

'Take My Breath Away' by Berlin – *Top Gun* (1986)

'King Of The Road' by Roger Miller – *Swingers* (1996)

'What A Wonderful World' by Louis Armstrong – *Good Morning, Vietnam* (1987)

'Love Is All Around' by Wet Wet Wet – *Four Weddings And A Funeral* (1994)

'Bohemian Rhapsody' by Queen – *Wayne's World* (1992)

'Into The Groove' by Madonna – *Desperately Seeking Susan* (1985)

'Eye Of The Tiger' by Survivor – *Rocky III* (1988)

'(Everything I Do) I Do It For You' by Bryan Adams – *Robin Hood: Prince Of Thieves* (1991)

'I Will Always Love You' by Whitney Houston – *The Bodyguard* (1992)

'Shoop Shoop Song (It's In His Kiss)' by Cher – *Mermaids* (1990)

'Green Onions' By Booker T And The MGs – *Get Shorty* (1995)

'Stuck In The Middle With You' by Stealer's Wheel – *Reservoir Dogs* (1992)

'My Heart Will Go On' by Celine Dion – *Titanic* (1997)

'Unchained Melody' by the Righteous Brothers – *Ghost* (1990)

'That's Amore' by Dean Martin – *Moonstruck* (1987)

'We Don't Need Another Hero' by Tina Turner – *Mad Max Beyond Thunderdome* (1985)

'Danger Zone' by Kenny Loggins – *Top Gun* (1986)

'Endless Love' by Diana Ross and Lionel Richie – *Endless Love* (1981)

'Moon River'by Henry Mancini – *Breakfast At Tiffany's* (1961)

'Stayin' Alive' by The Bee Gees – *Saturday Night Fever* (1977)

'Pretty In Pink' by The Psychedelic Furs – *Pretty In Pink* (1986)

— TEN THINGS YOU POSSIBLY DIDN'T KNOW — ABOUT...BJÖRK

- 'Björk' is the Icelandic name for 'birch tree.'
- Björk has a tattoo of a Viking compass on her arm.
- Björk's son, Sindri, is named after a dwarf who made Thor's hammer.
- Björk's favorite book is *Story Of The Eye* by George Bataillle.
- Björk has been taking shotokan karate classes for years.
- Björk touches her nose when she is nervous.
- Björk authored a book, *Um Urnot*, in 1984. She self published it and only handed out 100 copies.
- As a teenager, Björk performed in an all-girl punk band called Spit And Snot.
- In school, Björk always had crushes on the 'boys in the back of the classroom with really thick glasses and the bug collections'.
- Björk has worked in an antiques shop, a bookstore, a Coca-Cola bottling plant and a fish factory.

— UNFORTUNATE MUSICAL DEATHS —

Leslie Harvey (Stone The Crows) – electrocuted by his guitar – 1972

Merle Watson (guitarist) – tractor accident – 1985

Ramon Barrero (known for playing the world's smallest harmonica) – choked on his tiny instrument –1994

Terry Kath (Chicago) – Russian roulette – 1987

Jean-Baptiste Lully (conductor) – gangrene after spearing his toe with his conducting staff – 1687

Henry Purcell (composer) – chocolate poisoning – 1695

Stephen Foster (composer/songwriter) – fell from his bed – 1864

Johann Schobert (composer) – ate poisonous mushrooms – 1767

Ernest Chausson (composer) – rode bicycle into wall – 1899

— UNFORTUNATE MUSICAL DEATHS (CONTINUED) —

Graham Bond (The Graham Bond Organization) – fell to death under Tube train – 1974

Alban Berg (composer) – poisonous insect bite – 1935

César Franck (composer) – run over by trolley – 1890

Wallingford Riegger (composer) – died from head injuries after getting tangled in the leads of two fighting dogs – 1961

Anton Von Webern (composer) – accidentally shot by a sniper – 1945

Gustav Kobbe – seaplane landed on his boat – 1918

Allesandro Stadalla – assassinated – 1682

— INSTRUCTIONS FOR STOCKHAUSEN'S 'GOLDSTAUB' — (FROM *AUS DEM SIEBEN TAGEN* 1968)

Live completely alone for four days, without food, in complete silence without much movement. Sleep as little as necessary. Think as little as possible. After four days, late at night, play single sounds using only your intuition. Close your eyes, just listen.

— CRAZY COMPOSERS —

Gaetano Donizetti (1797-1848) – insanity/paralysis
Ivor Gurney (1890-1937) – schizophrenia
Lorenzo Perosi (1872-1956) – admitted to mental hospital
Robert Schumann (1810-56) – bipolar/self-starvation
Bedrich Smetana (1824-84) – deafness/mental disturbance
Jan Kritel Vanhal (1739-1813) – religious delusion
Hugo Wolf (1860-1903) – exhaustion/depression
Sergei Rachmaninoff (1873-1943) – depression
Peter Tchaikovsky (1840-1893) – insomnia/hallucinations
Ludwig Van Beethoven (1770-1827) – bipolar
Ivor Gurney (1890-1937) – manic depression

— MUSICIANS 5' 2" OR UNDER —

Dolly Parton – 4' 11"
Petula Clark – 5' 0"
Paul Anka – 5' 0"
Linda Ronstadt – 5' 2"
Stevie Nicks – 5' 1"
Paula Abdul – 5' 2"
Bushwick Bill – 4' 7"
Jennifer Love Hewitt – 5' 2"
Paul Simon – 5' 2"
Phife Dawg (A Tribe Called Quest) – 5' 1"
Bette Midler – 5' 1"
Prince – 5' 2"

— MUSIC-RELATED PHOBIAS —

Melophobia	Fear of music
Aulophobia	Fear of flutes
Chorophobia	Fear of dancing
Cyberphobia	Fear of computers or working on computers
Ligyrophobia	Fear of loud noises
Topophobia	Fear of performing (aka stage fright)
Acousticophobia	Fear of noise or sound
Theatrophobia	Fear of theatres
Glossophobia	Fear of speech
Verbophobia	Fear of words
Phonophobia	Fear of voices
Metrophobia	Fear of poetry

— MUSICIANS WHO HAVE GRACED *SESAME STREET* —

N Sync
Garth Brooks
The Goo Goo Dolls
Patti Labelle
Tracy Chapman
Johnny Cash
REM
Ray Charles
Faith Hill
James Taylor
Squirrel Nut Zippers
Paul Simon
Little Richard
Gloria Estefan
Kid 'N' Play
The Temptations
Celine Dion

— LEFT HANDERS —

Carl Philipp Emanuel Bach	David Byrne
Ludwig Van Beethoven	Kurt Cobain
Jimi Hendrix	Billy Corgan
Phil Collins	The Everly Brothers (both of them)
Paul McCartney	Glen Frey
Cole Porter	George Michael
Paul Simon	Robert Plant
Ringo Starr	Seal
Annie Lennox	Eminem
Glen Campell	

— DIRECTIONAL MICROPHONE RESPONSES —

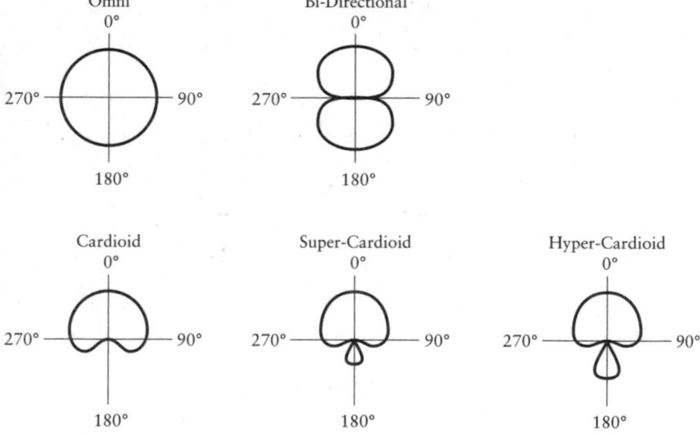

— CREATURE CURIOSITIES —

- Most cows give more milk when they listen to music.
- Giraffes have no vocal cords.
- Ducks' quacks don't echo.
- Some whales can stun their prey with sound.

- Cats can hear ultrasound.
- The hippopotamus does 80% of vocalisations under water.
- A nightingale can warble for up to 20 seconds without a breath.
- In still conditions, a thrush can be heard nearly a mile away.
- A cricket's song gets faster the warmer it is (count the number of chirps you hear in 14 seconds and then add 40 to calculate the current temperature).
- African heart-nosed bats can hear the footsteps of a beetle walking on sand from a distance of more than six feet.
- Crickets hear through their knees.
- The housefly hums in the key of F.
- Elephants communicate in sound waves too low for humans to hear.
- Termites eat twice as fast when exposed to loud music.
- Chickens lay the most eggs when pop music is played.
- The croak of a frog can change tones according to season.

— SONIC BOOMS —

Sonic booms are caused by an object moving faster than sound. There are two types of boom: n-waves and u-waves. The n-wave is generated from steady flight conditions, and has a pressure wave shaped like the letter n. The u-wave (aka focused boom), is generated from manoeuvering flights, and has a pressure wave shaped like the letter u. The strongest sonic boom ever recorded was 144lb per sq ft, produced by an F-4 flying just above the speed of sound at an altitude of 100ft.

— THE THREE TENORS —

Placido Domingo • Jose Carreras • Luciano Pavarotti

— CRIMINALLY MINDED —

Artist	Crime	Year	Sentence
Keith Richards	Allowing a house to be used for smoking cannabis	1967	1 year in jail, £500 ($300) fine
Jim Morrison	Drunk in public, indecent exposure	1969	Six months' labour, $500 (£300) fine
Mick Jagger	Unlawful possession of four benzedrine tablets	1977	Three months in jail
Siouxsie Sioux	Obstruction	1977	£20 ($16) fine
Sid Vicious	Charged with murdering girlfriend Nancy Spungen	1978	Died while on bail
Chuck Berry	Tax evasion	1979	Four months in jail, 1,000 hours' community service
Hugh Cornwell	Possession of drugs	1980	£300 ($550) fine, three months in jail
David Crosby	Possession of drugs and handgun	1982	1 year in jail
James Brown	Possession of drugs and firearms, aggravated assault and resisting arrest	1988	$6\frac{1}{2}$ years in jail
Bonnie Raitt	Civil disobedience	2001	$150 (£250) fine, three months' supervision
Johnny Cash	Amphetamine smuggling across the Mexican border	1965	Suspended sentence and fine.
Huddie Ledbetter	Murder and assault to kill	1917	30 years on a chain gang (completed seven)
Chuck Berry	Armed robbery		Three years an Algoa Reformatory
Red Hot Chili Peppers	Bassist Flea and drummer Chad Smith charged with battery and sexually		Apologise, pay a $1,000 (£650) fine, $5,000 (£3,000) to a

	harassing a woman in Daytona Beach, Florida		rape-crisis centre and $300 (£200) in prosecution costs.
Rick James	Assault on a woman	1994	Two-year prison sentence
Gary Glitter	Harbouring child pornography on his computer	1997	Four months in jail.
George Michael	Committing lewd act in Beverly Hills toilet	1998	$800 (£550) in fines, 80 hours' community service.

— THIS ONE GOES OUT TO... —

Performer	Song Title	Year	Dedicated To
Roberta Flack	'Killing Me Softly'	1973	Don McLean
Joe Cocker	'Delta Lady'	1990	Rita Coolidge
Carly Simon	'You're So Vain'	1972	Warren Beatty
Pink Floyd	'Shine On You Crazy Diamond'	1975	Syd Barret
Neil Sedaka	'Oh Carol'	1959	Carole King
The Rolling Stones	'Angie'	1973	Angie Bowie
Billy Joel	'Uptown Girl'	1983	Christie Brinkley
The Beatles	'Baby You're A Rich Man'	1967	Brian Epstein
Don McLean	'American Pie'	1971	Buddy Holly
Derek And The Dominos	'Layla'	1970	Patti Boyd
The Beatles	'Lady Madonna'	1968	Fats Domino
Fats Domino	'Lady Madonna'	1968	The Beatles
Stevie Wonder	'Sir Duke'	1976	Duke Ellington

— TWO WORLD RECORDS —

The largest production record made was a 21" format offered briefly by Thomas Edison. The smallest vinyl record ever made was a 2" record containing a reading of the Lord's prayer.

— SUICIDAL TENDENCIES —

Artist	Choice Of Suicide Weapon	Year
Michael Holliday	Gun	1963
Joe Meek	Gun	1967
Bobby Bloom	Gun	1974
Pete Ham	Noose	1975
Ian Curtis	Noose	1980
The Singing Nun	OD	1985
Richard Manuel	Noose	1986
Roy Buchanan	Noose	1988
Del Shannon	Gun	1990
Michael Hutchence	Noose	1997
Sid Vicious	OD	1979
Kurt Cobain	Gun	1994
Nick Drake	OD	1974
Paul Williams	Gun	1973

— THE FIVE POSITIONS OF THE FEET — IN CLASSICAL BALLET

Invented by Pierre/Charles Louis Beauchamp (1636-1705)

- Première Position: The feet form one line, heels touching one another.
- Seconde Position: The feet are on the same line but with a distance of about one foot between the heels.
- Troisième Position: One foot is in front of the other, heels touching the middle of the other foot.
- Quatrième Position: Similar to the third position, but with the feet parallel and separated by the length of one foot.*
- Cinquième Position: The Cecchetti method, where the feet are crossed so that the first joint of the big toe shows beyond either heel.*

* *In the French and Russian schools the feet are completely crossed so that the heel of the front foot touches the toe of the back foot and vice versa.*

— MEATLESS MUSICIANS —

Sara McLaughlin *Vegetarian*
Prince *Vegetarian*
Elvis Costello *Vegetarian*
Seal *Vegetarian*
Dizzy Gillespie *Vegetarian*
Meat Loaf *Vegetarian*
Ringo Starr *Vegetarian*
Annie Lennox *Vegetarian*
Paul McCartney *Vegetarian*
Lenny Kravitz *Vegetarian*
Ozzy Osbourne *Vegetarian*
Billy Idol *Vegetarian*
George Harrison *Vegetarian*
Peter Gabriel *Vegetarian*
Bob Dylan *Vegetarian*
'Weird' Al Yankovic *Vegan*
Fiona Apple *Vegan*
kd lang *Vegan*
Bryan Adams *Vegan*
Sinéad O'Connor *Vegan*
Moby *Vegan*
Steven Tyler *Vegan*
John and Yoko Lennon *Vegan*

— THE MANY MONIKERS OF JOHN LENNON —

Dr Winston O'Boogie • Long John • Dr Winston Booker Table • Dwarf McDougal • Rev Fred Ghurkin • Dr Winston O'Ghurkin • Musketeer Gripweed • Mel Torment • Dr Dream • Honarary John • St John Johnson • Dr Winston O'Reggae • John O'Cean • Joel Nohnn • Kaptain Kundalini • John F Lennon • Fred Zimmerman • John Green (when John was travelling) • Dr Winston • Rev Thumbs Ghurkin • Booker Table And The Maitre D's • Jock Lennon • Johnny Rhythm Honorary John St John Johnson

— OPTIGAN DISCS —

The Optigan (OPTIcal orGAN) was made by the toy manufacturer Mattel in the early '70s. Presented like an ordinary home organ of the time, it played not electronic sounds but specially made clear LP-sized discs optically encoded with looped recordings of real instruments and instrumental accompaniments. Each key on the 37-note keyboard triggered the record in the key chosen. Pressing the A minor chord button would play the installed record in a looped riff in A minor. Instead of grooves, the discs contained waveforms which were read by a light bar reader inside the Optigan. Volume was controlled with a foot pedal and the instrument also had switches for special effects, such as crowds cheering or monkeys whooping.

Optigan discs included: *Guitar Boogie*, *Champagne Music*, *Gospel Rock*, *Swing It!*, *Vox Humana*, *Cathedral Organ*, *Polka!*, *Mazurka!*, *Country Sunshine*, *Down Home*, *Country Waltz*, *New Orleans Blues*

— A SELECTION OF BLAXPLOITATION SOUNDTRACKS —

The Lost Man – Quincy Jones – 1969
Uptight – Booker T And The MGs – 1968
Shaft – Isaac Hayes – 1970
Trouble Man – Marvin Gaye – 1972
Black Caeser – James Brown/Fred Wesley – 1973
Hell Up In Harlem – Edwin Starr – 1973
Cool Breeze – Solomon Burke – 1972
Black Samson – Allen Toussaint – 1974
Cornbread, Earl And Me – Blackbyrds – 1975
Three The Hard Way – The Impressions – 1974
Together Brothers – Barry White – 1974
Foxy Brown – Willie Hutch – 1974
Across 110th Street – JJ Johnson And Bobby Womack – 1972

— ACRONYMS AND INITIALS OF — MUSICAL INSTITUTIONS

AURA	Association of United Recording Artists
APRS	Association of Professional Recording Services
BARD	British Association Of Record Dealers
BCC	British Copyright Council
BPI	British Phonographic Industry
BAC&S	British Academy of Composers and Songwriters
CLA	Copyright Licensing Agency
ERA	Educational Recording Agency Ltd
FACT	Federation Against Copyright Theft
IFPI	International Federation of the Phonographic Industry
IPI	Intellectual Property Institute
ISM	Incorporated Society of Musicians
MIA	Music Industries Association
MPA	Music Publishers Association
MPG	Music Producers Guild
MU	Musicians Union
NEAC	National Entertainment Agents Council
NMC	National Music Council
NMPA	National Music Publishers Association
PAMRA	Performing Arts Media Rights Association
RIAA	Recording Industry Association Of America

— CONCERTS YOU WISH YOU'D BEEN AT —

Bob Marley And The Wailers – The Lyceum – 1975

Elvis – Live In Hawaii ('Aloha From Hawaii') – 1973

Nirvana – MTV *Unplugged* In New York – 1994

Bob Dylan – Royal Albert Hall – 1966

The Doors – Dinner Key Auditorium in Coconut Grove (the 'Jim Exposed' concert) – 1969

Ozzy Osbourne – Iowa (the 'Bat Bites Back' concert) – 1982

The Beatles – *The Ed Sullivan Show* – 1964

Jimi Hendrix – Woodstock – 1969

The Rolling Stones – Altamont – 1969

— CONCERTS YOU WISH YOU'D BEEN AT (CONT'D) —

The Grateful Dead – Chicago (final performance) – 1995

Pink Floyd – The Dome, England
(first performance of *The Dark Side Of The Moon*) – 1972

David Bowie – London (final performance as
Ziggy Stardust And The Spiders From Mars) – 1973

The Band – San Francisco ('The Last Waltz') – 1976

The Who – San Francisco – 1973

Sinéad O'Connor – *Saturday Night Live* (the Pope-photo concert) – 1995

Lou Reed, Iggy Pop, The Ramones, Wendy O Williams and others –
Irving Plaza (unannounced) – 1986

Led Zeppelin – Los Angeles – 1977

— INDONESIAN KETJAK —

Ketjak singing, or the Ramayana Monkey Chant, is a traditional Indonesian chant performed by groups of 200 or more men, usually seated in concentric circles in a temple courtyard. The men are divided into groups, each chanting the syllable *tjak* in quick and successive volleys. The chant is ostensibly a re-enactment of the battle described in the Ramayana epic, in which monkey hordes come to the aid of Prince Rama in his battle with the evil King Ravana, though it is seen primarily as a dance of exorcism. The music has been likened to a rapid-fire game of table-tennis, where syllables are batted backwards and forwards instead of ping-pong balls.

— STEEL DRUMS —

According to Trinidadian legend, the original steel drum was created by a 12-year-old boy, Winston 'Spree' Simon (1930–1976). While growing up in Laventille, Spree was surrounded by factories that used – and discarded – tin drums. From these discards, Spree made a rudimentary 'kettle-drum', which he played in his local band. One day he loaned his instrument to a fellow band member, and when it was returned he found that much of its original convex playing surface had been beaten inward. It was while trying to reshape the pan from the inside with a stone that he discovered different sounds could be made from the various areas of the playing surface. He created a four-tone pan out of this happy accident and by 1943 had improved his pan's capacity to nine notes. In 1946 he came up with a 14-note version. Today there are around 1,000 steel bands worldwide.

— MUSIC COLLECTIONS OF INTEREST — AROUND THE WORLD

Athens, Greece – Museum of Popular Instruments, Research Centre for Ethnomusicology

Baku, Azerbaijan Republic – The State Museum of Azerbaijan Musical Culture

Basel, Switzerland – Musikmuseum, Historisches Museum Basel

Brussels, Belgium – Museum of Musical Instruments

Budapest, Hungary – Ferenc Liszt Memorial Museum

Budapest, Hungary – Budapest Music History Museum

Cleveland, Ohio, USA – Rock and Roll Hall of Fame

Copenhagen, Denmark – Musikhistorisk Museet

The Hague, The Netherlands – Gemeentemuseum

Hull, Quebec, Canada – Canadian Museum of Civilization

Kent, England – Finchcocks Museum of Music

Kremsmuenster, Austria – Streitwieser Brass Instrument Collection, Schloss Kremsegg Castle

La Couture Boussey, France – Musée des Instruments à Vent

Leipzig, Germany – Musikinstrumenten-Museum der Universität Leipzig

Lisbon, Portugal – Museu da Música

London, England – The Horniman Museum

London, England – The Royal Academy of Music, York Gate Collections

London, England – Royal College of Music Museum of Instruments

— MUSIC COLLECTIONS OF INTEREST — AROUND THE WORLD (CONTINUED)

Manchester, England – Royal Northern College of Music Collection of Historic Musical Instruments

Markneukirchen, Germany – Museum of Musical Instruments

Montluçon, France – Musée des Musiques Populaires de Montlucçon

Moscow, Russia – Glinka State Museum of Musical Culture

Neuchâtel, Switzerland – Musée d'Ethnographie

New York, New York, USA – The Metropolitan Museum of Art

Nürnberg, Germany – Germanisches Nationalmuseum

Opatówek, Poland – Museum of Industrial History

Oxford, England – The Bate Collection, University of Oxford

Oxford, England – Pitt Rivers Museum, University of Oxford

Paris, France – Musée de la Musique, Cité de la Musique

Poznan, Poland – Museum of Musical Instruments

Quebec, Canada – Canadian Museum of Civilization

St Petersburg, Russia – The Museum of Musical Instruments

Seattle, Washington, USA – Experience Music Project

Stockholm, Sweden – The Nydahl Collection

Stockholm, Sweden – The Stockholm Music Museum

Tokyo, Japan – Collection for Organology, Kunitachi College of Music

Trondheim, Norway – Ringve Museum

Turku, Finland – The Sibelius Museum

Vermillion, South Dakota, USA – National Music Museum

Vienna, Austria – Sammlung alter Musikinstrumente, Kunsthistorisches Museum

Washington, DC, USA – Library of Congress Collections of Musical Instruments

Washington, DC, USA – National Museum of American History, Smithsonian Institution

— SPICE GIRLS STATS —

Real Name	Spice Name	Star Sign	Fave Breakfast
Emma Bunton	Baby Spice	Aquarius	Scrambled eggs
Dislikes: Liars			
Worst Injury: Run over by a car			
Victoria Adams	Posh Spice	Aries	Sugar Puffs
Dislikes: English People Who Complain About The Weather			
Worst Injury: Meningitis			
Melanie Chisolm	Sporty Spice	Capricorn	Pizza
Dislikes: Snot and Steps			
Worst Injury: Spiral fracture on foot bone			
Melanie Brown	Scary Spice	Gemini	Bacon sandwich
Dislikes: Liars and false-minded people			
Worst Injury: Broke both kneecaps			
Geri Halliwell	Ginger Spice	Leo	Salmon
Dislikes: Bad smells, men who treat women badly			
Worst Injury: Unknown			

— HOW TO PLAY THE TAMBOURINE (STEP BY STEP) —

- Hold instrument horizontally in your weaker hand
- Place thumb on top of the head and other four fingers underneath.
- Bring your strong hand to the tambourine and slap the head to produce a clear, crisp sound.
- To produce a roll, begin with a slap from your strong hand then shake the tambourine in a brisk, quick back-and-forth manner to sustain it.
- The thumb roll is achieved by rubbing the head of the tambourine around the edge to cause the jingles to vibrate.

* *To add some variation, try striking the tambourine with your fist, elbow, knee, head, or even your face.*

— NOTABLE EARLY MUSIC DICTIONARIES —

Johannes Tinctoris – *Terminorum Musicae Diffinitorium* – 1473
Jean-Jacques Rousseau – *Dictionnaire de Musique* – 1764
Charles Burney – *A General History Of Music* – 1782 – 89
Heinrich Christoph Koch – *Musikalishes Lexikon* – 1802
FJ Fetis – *Biographie Universelle des Musiciens* – 1868
Hugo Riemann – *Musik-Lexikon* – 1882
John Moore – *Musician's Lexicon* – 1845*
Sir George Grove – *Dictionary Of Music And Musicians* – 1879–89
Theodore Baker – *Biographical Dictionary Of Musicians* – 1900

**First American music encyclopedia*

TEN BEATLES SONGS — PRODUCED BY GEORGE MARTIN —

'Hey Jude'	Apple	1968
'I Want To Hold Your Hand'	Capitol	1964
'Can't Buy Me Love'	Capitol	1964
'A Hard Day's Night'	Capitol	1964
'Come Together'	Apple	1969
'All You Need Is Love'	Capitol	1967
'Yellow Submarine'	Capitol	1968
'Nowhere Man'	Capitol	1966
'Strawberry Fields Forever'	Capitol	1967
'Please Please Me'	Vee Jay	1964

— CHILD BALLADS —

Between 1882 and 1898, Francis James Child, a professor of Rhetoric and English Literature at Harvard University (1851–1896), published *The English And Scottish Popular Ballads*, a five-volume collection of traditional ballads. The compilation took him more than two decades to complete and remain the definitive collection of the story-telling song tradition. Between 1963 and 1968, Bertrand Bronson, a Stanford University scholar, collected the music to go with Child's texts, and the complete anthology was named *The Child's Ballads*, after its original collector.

— THE LARGEST INTERNATIONAL MUSIC FESTIVAL — IN THE WORLD

WOMAD – World Of Music, Arts and Dance – was started in 1982 by pop star Peter Gabriel. To date there have been more than 90 events in 20 different countries, with an estimated 1,500 international artists presented to a live audience of over 1 million people. Countries and islands that have hosted the event include Australia, Austria, Canada, Canary Islands, Czech Republic, Denmark, Estonia, Finland, France, Germany, Greece, Guernsey, Italy, Japan, New Zealand, Portugal, Sardinia, Sicily, Singapore, South Africa, Spain, Sweden, Turkey, the USA and the UK.

— SOME DOO WOP SONGS —

The Valentines	'Woo Woo Train'	1955 (Rama)
The Rivingtons	'Pa Pa Ooh Mow Mow'	1962 (Liberty)
The Moonglows	'Shoo Doo Be Doo (My Lovin' Baby)'	1954 (Chess)
The Silhouettes	'Bing Bong'	1957 (Ember Records)
Bob Crewe	'Do Be Do Be Do'	1957 (Vik)
The Squires	'Do Be Oo Be Wop Wop'	1960 (Vita)
The Five Daps	'Do Whop-A-Do'	1958 (Brax)
The Twilighters	'Wah Bop Sh Wah'	1955 (Specialty)
Davey And The Doo Drops	'Do Dee Do Dee Do Wah'	1958 (Guyden)
The Spaniels	'Do-Wah'	1955 (Vee Jay)
Lew Williams	'Bop Bop Ba Doo Bop'	1956 (Imperial)

— THE LIMBERJACK —

The Limberjack – sometimes called a clogger man, jigger or a shuffling Sam – is a wooden doll-like figure attached to a stick that creates rhythms as it dances. Though known as an Appalachian mountain instrument, the Limberjack originated in the British Isles several hundred years ago as a way of imitating clog dancers.

— STYLES OF THE CARIBBEAN —

Cuba Son, Rumba, Mambo, Punto • **Dominican Republic** Merengue • **Puerto Rico** Salsa, Bomba, Plena, Merengue, Jiharo • **Jamaica** Reggae, Ska, Dancehall, Rocksteady, Dub • **Trinidad And Tobago** Calypso, Soca, Tamboo Bamboo • **Martinique And Guadeloupe** Zouk • **Haiti** Cadance, Merengue • **Venezuela** Merengue

THE DEATH ROW MIXTAPE — (MUSIC TO AWAIT TRIAL TO) —

Dr Dre 'Stranded On Death Row' (1989)
Snoop Doggy Dog 'Murder Was The Case' (1994)
2Pac '16 On Death Row' (1997)
Judas Priest 'Death Row' (1997)
Accept 'Death Row' (1995)
Prince 'Electric Chair' (1989)
Queensrÿche 'Electric Requiem' (1988)
Killing Joke 'Requiem' (1980)
Nick Cave 'The Mercy Seat' (1988)
Johnny Cash '25 Minutes To Go' (1965)
Bruce Springsteen 'Dead Man Walking' (1996)
Led Zeppelin 'Gallows Pole' (1970)
Hank Williams 'I'll Never Get Out of This World Alive' (1952)
The Kingston Trio 'Tom Dooley' (1958)

— A CAPPELLA —

The phrase *a cappella* (often misspelled as *a capella*, *a capela* or *a cappela*') is Italian in origin and means 'in the church style' or, more specifically, 'in the style of the chapel'. Today it is today taken to mean an arrangement for unaccompanied voices, although instruments may be used to double the vocal parts. If an electric bass is used to strengthen the vocal bass line, for example, the piece would still be *a cappella*.

— HAYDN'S NAMED SYMPHONIES —

Franz Joseph Haydn (1732–1809) is known as the father of the symphony. During his career he wrote 104 of them, almost 30 of which were given nicknames. The names were usually given by Haydn himself, but also by the publicist of the work and sometimes by the audience.

6 in D: Le Matin
7 in C: Le Midi
8 in G: Le Soir
22 in E♭: The Philosopher
26 in D minor: Lamentatione
30 in C: Alleluia
31 in D: Horn Signal
43 in E flat: Mercury
44 in E minor: Trauer
45 in F♯ minor: Farewell
48 in C: Maria Theresa
49 in F minor: La Passione
53 in D: Imperial
55 in E♭: Schoolmaster
59 60 in C: Il Distratto
63 in C: La Roxelane
69 in C: Laudon
73 in D: La Chasse
82 in C: The Bear
83 in G minor: The Hen
85 in B♭: The Queen
92 in G: Oxford
94 in G: The Surprise
96 in D: The Miracle
100 in G: Military
101 in D minor: The Clock
103 in E♭ :The Drum Roll
104 in D: London

* *Haydn was buried just outside Eisenstadt to avoid the attention of Napoleon's troops, who were occupying the city at the time. A few days after his burial, it was decreed that his remains be exhumed and reburied in the city. When the coffin was opened, Haydn's head appeared to be missing. The skull was anonymously returned to the Society of Music Lovers in Austria in 1954 and finally reunited with his body.*

— GRAPH OF DECIBEL RATINGS —

The unit of sound amplitude is the *bel*, named in honour of American inventor Alexander Graham Bell. It is a unit that expresses the logarithmic ratio between the input and output of any given component, circuit or system and may be expressed in terms of voltage, current, or power.

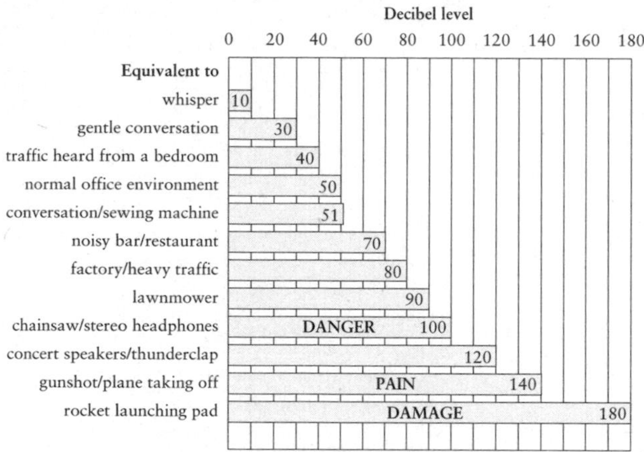

— TEN CLASSICS PENNED BY GEORGE GERSHWIN —

'But Not For Me' (1930)
'I've Got A Crush On You' (1930)
'Fascinating Rhythm' (1924)
'S'Wonderful' (1927)
'Let's Call The Whole Thing Off' (1937)
Rhapsody In Blue (1924)
Porgy And Bess (1935)
'Summertime' (1935)
'Embraceable You' (1930)
'I Got Rhythm' (1934)

— TONE POEMS —

Tone poem – a shorter name for the symphonic poem – is a phrase coined and first applied by Franz Liszt (1811–1886), who created the term to describe pieces written for textual materials that included narratives, settings or stories, plays or excerpts from stories or plays. Performances were accompanied by a programme which the audience member was able to read before the music started. Musically, the composition could be related to the text in a number of ways, none of which were necessarily literal. Numerous composers have used tone poems in the course of their writing, but the most extensive composer to maintain coherence in this form was Richard Strauss, who composed lengthy but realistic 'scenes' in his musical poetry. Some examples of tone poems:

Richard Strauss: *Don Juan*; *Also Sprach Zarathustra*; *Don Quixote*
Jean Sibelius: *Finlandia*; *En Saga*; *The Bard*
Hector Berlioz: *Romeo et Juliette*
Pyotr Tchaikovsky: *1812 Overture*; *The Tempest*
Franz Liszt: *A Faust Symphony*
Paul Dukas: *The Sorcerer's Apprentice*
Camille Saint-Saëns: *Bacchanale*

— COMB MUSIC BY G BRECHT (1959-1962) —

Instructions For A Single Or Multiple Performance

A comb is held by its spine in one hand, either free or resting on an object.

The thumb or a finger on the other hand is held with its tip against the end prong of a comb, with the edge of the nail overlapping the end of a prong.

The finger is slowly and uniformly moved so that the prong is inevitably released, and the nail engages the next prong.

This action is repeated until each prong has been used.

— BRASS TUBING LENGTHS —

Trombone	9' of tubing
Tuba	13'–14' of tubing
French horn	12'–13' of tubing
Trumpet	4'–5' of (compactly wrapped) tubing

— THE BASIC CONCEPTS OF INDIAN CANARTIC MUSIC —

The classical music of Southern India is called Canartic music, in reference of the southern state of Karnataka. The music in this area is almost wholly unified, with the different schools using the same ragas as a base, as well as the same solo rhythm instruments.

Sruti (key or pitch)
Raga (melody)
Laya (rhythm)
Sahitya (compositions)

**The Musical Trinity of Canartic music are Swami Tyagaraja, Muttu Sswami Dikshitar, and Shyama Sastri. They all lived about 150 years ago and were all born at Tiruvarur, in the Tanjavur district of Tamil Nadu.*

— CLAQUES —

Taken from the French word *claquer*, 'to clap', a claque is body of hired applauders. The concept stratches back as far as Roman times; it is recorded that Emperor Nero hired thousands of Roman soldiers (called Angustals) to cheer and applaud when he acted. The first professional claque organization, L'Assurance de Succès Dramatiques, was set up in Paris in the 1800s by a pair of opera lovers called Sauton and Porcher. Their 'claqueurs' were divided into different groups: 'commissaires', who would noisily pointe out a play's merits; 'rieurs', who laughed loudly at the funny parts; 'pleureurs', people (mainly women) who pretended to be upset during emotional scenes; 'chatouilleurs', who made amusing quips and gestures (from the French *chatouiller*, 'to tickle'); and finally the 'bisseurs', whose job was to shout 'Bis!' ('Encore!') at the end of a performance.

— ENTARTETE MUSIK —

Entartete Musik was an exhibit held in Düsseldorf in 1938 by the Nazi Party. The aim was to defame music that was considered 'degenerate'. This included atonal and jazz music, along with any works by Jews, homosexuals, communists, the mentally ill, gypsies and blacks. Most of the musicians, composers, musicologists and teachers listed in the exhibit were either forced to emigrate or were killed. They included:

Walter Braunfels • Berthold Goldschmidt • Pavel Haas • Erich Korngold • Hans Krasa • Ernst Krenek • Viktor Ullmann • Hans Eisler • Emmerich Kalman • Alexander Zemlinsky • Felix Mendelssohn • Karol Rathaus • Fritz Berens • Wilhelm Grosz • Arnold Schoenberg • Erwin Schulhoff • Franz Shreker • Paul Hindemith • Kurt Weill.

— SOCA —

Soca (originally named 'solka'), a fusion of calypso with Indian rhythms, combined the musical traditions of the two major ethnic groups of Trinidad and Tobago. The style was invented by Lord Shorty (height 6' 4"), who aimed to inject some new life into the flagging calypso scene and make a music that was more libidinous and larger than life. He first showcased his new hybrid on the song 'Cloak And Dagger' in 1963. By the 1980s, Lord Shorty became disenchanted with the style and underwent a huge change of heart. In 1981, he converted to Rastafarianism, changed his name to Ras Shorty I, and moved into a forest in southern Trinidad, where he continued to write songs of a more spiritual and political nature.

— TYPES OF CADENCE —

Perfect
Tonic chord preceded by a dominant chord.

Plagal
Tonic chord preceded by a subdominant chord.

Imperfect
Dominant chord preceded by any other chord.

Interrupted (Deceptive or False)
Dominant chord not followed by the expected tonic chord, but often by another chord.

— THE NOBLEMEN'S AND GENTLEMEN'S — CATCH CLUB OF LONDON

The Nobleman's And Gentlemen's Catch Club of London was founded in 1761 to encourage the composition of catches – songs with a single melody which, when sung at offset intervals by more than one person, provide their own harmonies. Modern examples of catches include 'Row, Row, Row Your Boat' and 'Three Blind Mice', though the ones that became popular between the late 16th and 19th centuries were much more humorous and ribald and were usually performed by three or more men.

— HOW TO BELLY DANCE AT HOME (STEP BY STEP) —

- Play a song with a strong beat.
- Walk briskly around, swaying your hips from side to side.
- Gracefully bring your arms out to each side.
- Raise arms into a 'V' that points diagonally toward the sky.
- Raise both hands directly overhead and relax the elbows just a little to create a soft curve.
- Keeping one arm overhead, drop the other so that your arms form a letter 'L'.
- Do the letter 'L' on the other side.
- Invent additional arm poses and movements that look graceful.
- To make a roll of the belly, contract the diaphragm and then the lower abdomen.
- Push the diaphragm out, followed by the lower abdomen.
- When you have enough control over that, smooth it out to a roll.
- Do this repeatedly until it looks like something in your stomach is rolling down.

— MUSIC BOXES —

Mechanical music boxes began in earnest in the 14th century with the development of the carillon in the Benelux countries of Europe. The automatic carillon of this era usually comprised bells that were struck by automatic hammers in church steeples. The modern music box traces its origins to tiny players hidden inside Swiss watches and snuff boxes in the 18th century. Because each of these cylinders was small and needed to be made by hand, the German 19th-century innovation of using interchangeable discs to hold the music program became quite popular. It was only the need to use production metal for World War I rather than music boxes that brought on the demise of the format. Players that used paper rolls instead of metal discs and cylinders – such as the 19th-century Celestinas, popular in America – helped to spread this early mechanically reproduced music far and wide, but it was eventually eclipsed by the phonograph.

— NOTES ON A PIANO —

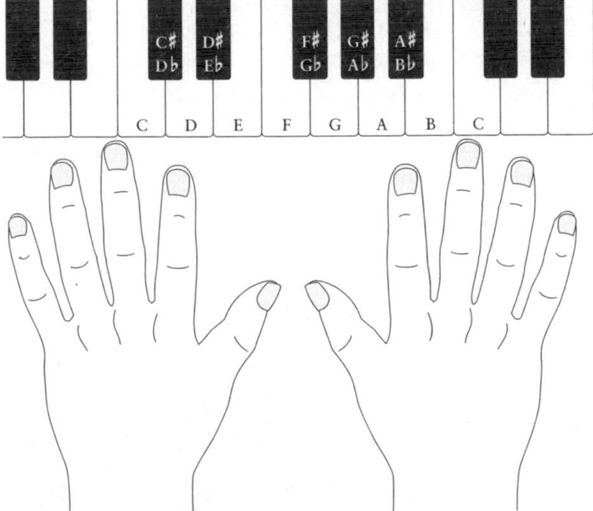

— FILM SOUNDTRACKS FEATURING THE THEREMIN —

The Theremin was invented by Russian physicist named Lev Sergeivitch Termen (anglicised to Leon Theremin). The instrument was originally patented in the US on 28 February 1928 as the 'thereminvox'. In addition to being used in many film sound tracks, it was popularised as a serious solo instrument played by the virtuoso Clara Rockmore.

Spellbound (dir Alfred Hitchcock, 1944)
The Lost Weekend (dir Billy Wilder, 1945)
Rocketship X-M (dir Kurt Neumann, 1950)
The Thing (dir Christian Nyby, 1951)
The Day The Earth Stood Still (dir Robert Wise, 1951)
The Ten Commandments (dir Cecil B De Mille, 1956)
Billy The Kid Vs Dracula (dir William Beaudine, 1966)
It Came From Outer Space (dir Jack Arnold, 1953)
The Queen Of Outer Space (dir Edward Bernds, 1958)
The Delicate Delinquent (dir Don Mcguire, 1957)
The Red House (dir Delmer Daves, 1947)
Ed Wood (dir Tim Burton, 1994)
Mars Attacks! (dir Tim Burton, 1996)
Bride Of Frankenstein (dir James Whale, 1935)
The Spiral Staircase (dir Robert Siodmak, 1946)
The Thing (dir John Carpenter, 1982)
Forbidden Planet (dir Fred M Wilcox, 1956)

— LIMBO —

It is widely believed that the roots of limbo may lie in the unhappy circumstances of the slave era. Scholars posit that following long, cramped trips, with feet and hands chained to metal bars, slaves developed a competitive exercise in which they attempted to pass under the bar without it touching their bodies. Whatever the roots of this distinctive – and these days jovial – music and dance ritual, the craze reached a zenith when Chubby Checker sold a million copies of song 'The Limbo Rock'.

* *One of the limbo world records is held by a young boy from Bombay, India, who managed to roller-skate under a pole only eight inches high.*

— JUILLIARD GRADUATES —

New York's Juilliard School, one of the world's most famous music schools, was founded in 1905 as the Institute of Musical Art by Dr Frank Damrosch (godson of Franz Liszt). In 1924, the Juilliard Graduate School was formed to help worthy music students complete their education. Alumni include:

Robin Williams • Paul Taylor • James Levine • Leontyne Price • Christine Babranski • Marcia Cross • Thomas Gibson • Brad Whitford • Kevin Kline • Kelsey Grammer • Itzhak Perlman • Miles Davies • Philip Glass • Van Cliburn • Richard Rodgers • Yo-Yo Ma • Lar Lubovitch • Renée Fleming • Teo Macero • Bob Berg • Steve Grossman • Pete Yellin • Eddie Damiels • Phil Woods • David Tofani • Wynton Marsalis • Julius Baker • Jeanne Baxtresser • Carol Wincenc • Stanley Drucker.

— 2002'S RICHEST MUSICIANS —

1. Paul McCartney – $72.1 million (£50 million)
2. The Rolling Stones – $44 million (£31 million)
3. The Dave Matthews Band – $31.3 million (£24 million)
4. Celine Dion – $31.1 million (£24 million)
5. Eminem – $28.9 million (£21 million)

Next five: Cher, Bruce Springsteen, Mariah Carey, Jay-Z, Ozzy Osbourne.

— SOME POPULAR DANCES OF THE '60s AND '70s —

The Twist, The Jerk, The Monkey, The Pony, The Swim, The Mashed Potato, The Skate, The Hitchhiker, The Egyptian, The Shimmy, The Temptation Walk, The Locomotion, The Street Hustle, The Latin Hustle, The Night Fever, The Line Dance, The Bus Stop, The Four Corners, The Bump, The Watusi, The Frug, The Funky Chicken, The Foxy Trot, The Tango Hustle

— TEN THINGS YOU POSSIBLY DIDN'T KNOW — ABOUT...EMINEM

- Eminem wanted to be a comic-book artist.
- When Eminem worked as a cook, he used to rap customers' orders to entertain his friends.
- Eminem's 2000 album, *The Marshall Mathers LP*, sold 1.76 million copies in the first week of release in the US – a record for a solo artist.
- Eminem refuses to use the word 'nigger' in any of his songs.
- When he was nine years old, Eminem suffered a series of beatings at elementary school that led to a week-long coma.
- When Eminem writes his lyrics, he starts at the corner of the paper and writes downward instead of writing on the lines.
- A 12-year-old girl came out of a coma after hearing Eminem through a set of headphones.
- Eminem has a twin sister named Dawn.
- Eminem's greatest fear is that a crazed fan will kill him at a concert.
- Eminem's tattoo artist is called Mr Cartoon and lives in California.

— LES SIX —

In 1920, a group of French composers comprising Georges Auric, Louis Durey, Arthur Honegger, Darius Milhaud, Francis Poulenc, and Germaine Tailleferre came together under the motivating influence of Jean Cocteau (with Erik Satie as a spiritual godfather) to create a style of purely French music. The group was christened 'Les Six' by critic Henri Collet, after the Russian 'Mighty Five'. Although all part of the same group, their musical styles were very diverse and they were often very critical of each other's work. They never managed to produce a collective work as such, but they nonetheless remained together as a group of friends and artists until 1924.

— FOUR SEASONAL ANTIPHONS SUNG IN HONOUR — OF THE BLESSED VIRGIN MARY

Regina Coeli • *Ave Regina Caelorum*
Alma Redemptoris Mater • *Salve, Regina*

— TEN CLASSICS PENNED BY COLE PORTER —

'Easy To Love' (1936)
'In The Still Of The Night' (1928)
'So In Love' (1948)
'Who Wants To Be A Millionaire' (1956)
'I Love Paris' (1953)
'I Get A Kick Out Of You' (1934)
'Night And Day' (1932)
'Anything Goes' (1934)
'I've Got You Under My Skin' (1936)
'Every Time We Say Goodbye' (1944)

— FIRST OF THE POPS —

The first broadcast of *Top Of The Pops* was in 1964. It was presented by Jimmy Savile and opened by The Rolling Stones, who sang 'I Wanna Be Your Man'.

— NUMBER ONE ON 1—

The first broadcast from BBC Radio 1 was in 1967. It was introduced by Tony Blackburn and the first record was 'Flowers In The Rain' by The Move.

— SIX BASIC STEPS OF HULA —

Koholo • Ka'o • Kawelu • Kahela • 'Ami • Lele

— SOME BANDS WITH AMERICAN PLACES — IN THEIR NAMES

Alabama, America, American Hi-Fi, American Music Club, American Tourist, At The Drive-In, Babylon Zoo, The Beach Boys, The Beautiful South, Big Country, The Boomtown Rats, Boston, Broadway, Brownsville Station, Caesar's Palace, Casino Drive, The Casinos, Chicago, Columbia, Confederate Railroad, Death In Vegas, Dirty Vegas, John Denver, Edison Lighthouse, Firehouse, 'Tennessee' Ernie Ford, Frankie Goes To Hollywood, Grant Lee Buffalo, David Houston, Highway 101, Jay And The Americans, Stonewall Jackson, Kansas, The Kentucky Headhunters, LA, LA Guns, Little Texas, Linkin Park, Minnesota Fats, New York Ska Jazz Ensemble, Rich Springfield, Texas, Texas Is The Reason, The Texas Tornados, Trout Fishing In America, Uncle Tupelo, The Village People, Woodstock.

— SOME MUSICIANS WITH HEARING DIFFICULTIES —

Neil Young
John Entwistle
Jeff Beck (Yardbirds)
Thom Yorke (Radiohead)
George Harrison
Cher
Ludwig Van Beethoven
Francis Rossi
Joey Kramer
Barbra Streisand
Engelbert Humperdinck
Sting
Lemmy (Motörhead)
Bono (U2)
Ozzy Ozborne
Robert Schumann
Kathy Peck
Lee Renaldo
Bob Mould
Pete Townshend
Brian Wilson
Eric Clapton
George Martin
Phil Collins
Huey Lewis
Charlie Haden
John Lee Hooker
Thurston Moore

— THE US AIR FORCE HYMN —

Lord, guard and guide the men who fly
Through the great spaces of the sky;
Be with them traversing the air
In darkening storms or sunshine fair.
Thou who dost keep with tender might
The balanced birds in all their flight;
Thou of the tempered winds be near
That, having thee, they know no fear,
Control their minds with instinct fit
What time, adventuring, they quit
The firm security of land;

Grant steadfast eye snd skilful hand
Aloft in solitudes of space,
Uphold them with thy saving grace.
O God, protect the men who fly
Thru lonely ways beneath the sky.

— MTV MISCELLANY —

- The first video to premiere on MTV was, appropriately, 'Video Killed The Radio Star' by Buggles, on 1 August 1981.
- The most aired video in MTV's history is Peter Gabriel's 'Sledgehammer'.
- MTV globally reaches upwards of 350 million households.
- Eighty-two per cent of MTV viewers are 12–34-years-old. Of those, 39 per cent are under the age of 18.
- MTV's original five veejays were Martha Quinn, Nina Blackwood, Mark Goodman, JJ Jackson and Alan Hunter.
- A quarter of all MTV videos depict alcohol or tobacco use and overt violence.
- MTV is received in 140 countries worldwide.
- MTV is the most valuable individual media brand in the world, with an estimated value of $6.6 billion (£4.6 billion).
- MTV was initially put on the air as an inexpensive way to fill a gap in regional cable programming.
- Until 31 March 1983, MTV showed only videos of white artists. On that day they premiered 'Beat It' by Michael Jackson.
- The New World Teen Study found that teens who watch MTV are more likely than other teens to wear the 'teen uniform' of jeans, running shoes and denim jacket, to own electronics and to consume fast food and personal-care products.

— SOME FAMOUS OPERA HOUSES —

Vienna State Opera House	Austria
La Scala	Milan
The Metropolitan	New York
Palais Garnier	Paris
Sydney Opera House	Sydney
The Royal Opera House	London
Colon Theater	Buenos Aires
Bayreuth Festspielhaus	Bayreuth
Arena	Verona
Opera Garnier De Monte-Carlo	Monaco
Glyndebourne	UK
Semper Opera House	Dresden
Cairo Opera House	Egypt

— AN ENCHANTING READ —

The *Liber Usaulis* ('The Usual Book') is the most complete book of chant available for the Tridentine rites. It contains all of the chants for every feast of the year as well as all special services, such as burials, weddings, blessing of Holy Oils, ordinations and benedictions. The volume also contains the common chants for the Divine Office and the ordinary chants for the Mass.

— TEN SONGS PENNED BY PRINCE FOR OTHER PEOPLE —

Sinéad O'Connor – 'Nothing Compares 2 U' – Ensign 1990
Chaka Khan – 'I Feel For You' – Warner Bros – 1984
The Bangles – 'Manic Monday' – Columbia 1986
MC Hammer – 'Pray' – Capitol 1990
Tevin Campbell – 'Round and Round' – Paisley Park 1991
Sheila E – 'A Love Bizarre' – Paisley Park 1986
Sheena Easton – 'Sugar Walls' – EMI America 1985
Martika – 'Love...Thy Will Be Done' – Columbia 1991
'Paul Abdul' – U – Virgin 1991

**Prince's pseudonyms include Jamie Starr, Alexander Nevermind, Christopher Tracy, Madhouse and Paisley Park.*

— COPYRIGHT FACTS —

1. A work does not have to be registered to be copyrighted; the © emblem no longer has to be present to designate something that is copyrighted.
2. Copyright lasts the entirety of the author's lifetime, and then an additional 70 years past that, after which it then belongs to the author's heirs.
3. Work done in the course of employment, or work that is published under a pseudonym or anonymously, is copyrighted for 95–120 years, depending on the date the work was published.
4. The primary goal of copyright law is 'to promote the progress of science and the useful arts'.
5. The copyright holder possesses the following rights in relation to his/her own work: the right to reproduce it, perform it or display it publicly, to prepare derivative works from it, and the right to distribute and copy it.
6. Creative ideas are not protected.
7. Music and sound on the internet, including wave and MIDI sequencing, are copyrighted.
8. MIDI files can be copyrighted by any and all of the following: the composer, the lyricist, the MIDI sequencer, the record company, and/or the publisher.
9. 'Fair Use' rule – use of another's copyrighted work is available to the public on a limited basis, usually in the form of criticism and comment, reporting and news, research, non-profit educational use, or parody.
10. Information that is in the public domain includes work where the copyright has expired or been abandoned, information created by the government, or work that is not considered copyrightable, such as facts, ideas, titles, etc.

— THE GETAWAY MIXTAPE (MUSIC TO TRAVEL TO) —

Marty Robbins	'El Paso'	Columbia 1960
Eagles	'Hotel California'	Asylum 1977
Toto	'Africa'	Columbia 1983
Kenny Ball And His Jazzmen	'Midnight In Moscow'	Kapp 1962
The Beatles	'Penny Lane'	Capitol 1967
Men At Work	'Down Under'	Columbia 1983
Murray Head	'One Night In Bangkok'	RCA 1985
David Bowie	'Little China Girl'	EMI America 1983
Harry Belafonte	'Jamaica Farewell'	RCA 1957
Three Dog Night	'Never Been To Spain'	Dunhill 1972

— SOME COLOURED NOISES AND THEIR FREQUENCIES —

Grey Noise – 7–500Hz
Green Noise – 500–2000Hz
Black Noise – Above 20,000Hz
White Noise – 18–22,000Hz
Pink Noise – 18–10,000Hz
Blue Noise – 10,000–22,000 Hz

— PIERRE SCHAEFFER'S SEVEN CATEGORIES OF SOUND —

*Pierre Scaeffer is regarded as the first person to use tape for musical composition. He invented the term *musique concrète* to describe his first electronic studies.

Mass • Dynamic • Harmonic Timbre
Melodic Profile • Mass Profile
Gain • Inflection.

— TEN CLASSICS PENNED BY BURT BACHARACH — AND HAL DAVID

'(There's) Always Something There To Remind Me', 1964, Sandie Shaw
'Do You Know The Way To San Jose', 1967, Dionne Warwick
'I Just Don't Know What To Do With Myself', 1962, Tommy Hunt
'I Say A Little Prayer', 1966, Aretha Franklin

'The Look Of Love', 1967, Dusty Springfield
'Magic Moments', 1957, Perry Como
'Raindrops Keep Fallin' On My Head', 1969, BJ Thomas
'Walk On By', 1964, Dionne Warwick
'I'll Never Fall In Love Again', 1968, Dionne Warwick
'House Is Not A Home', 1964, Brenton Brook

SCHOENBERG'S RULES FOR — 12-TONE COMPOSITION —

Arnold Schoenberg (1874-1951) was one of the founders of 12-tone (serial) music, in which all 12 notes of the chromatic scale have equal importance.

The row, or series, must contain all 12 pitch-classes of the chromatic scale in a specific and predetermined order with no repetitions of any one pitch class.

The permissible row forms include a row's original or prime form, inversion, retrograde and retrograde inversion, and the 12 transpositions of each. The total number of row forms, or permutations, is 48 and can be represented concisely in a form of chart called a *matrix*.

Consistently atonal treatment of the row requires that no notes be doubled at the octave, tonal melodic or harmonic elements (intervals) are to be avoided, and no note should be sustained to the point where it becomes a focal pitch.

In order to maintain uniformity of musical material, one must make exclusive use of one series per composition.

— FENDER FACTS —

Leo Fender worked as an accountant and radio repairman before taking up music-instrument manufacturing during World War II.

- Fender makes more than 1,000 guitars a day.
- Red, white, sunburst and black are the most popular Fender colours.
- A Fender fan from Lancashire, England, created a life-sized Fender guitar out of 7,000 matchsticks.
- Fender guitars were not designed as rock 'n' roll machines. Fenders were around several years before the explosion of rock 'n' roll. The music was shaped by the equipment, not the reverse.
- The Fender Telecaster (originally called the Broadcaster), introduced in 1951, was the first solid body electric Spanish-style guitar ever to go into commercial production.
- In 1995, guitar fan Chris Black of London held a wedding ceremony to marry officially his Fender Stratocaster.
- In their last 'concert' on the roof of Apple Headquarters in the movie *Let It Be*, The Beatles' entire backdrop was fashioned from Fender amps.
- Unable to locate large quantities of vacuum tubes for its tube amplifiers, Fender once enlisted the help of the Russian government to increase the quality of tubes made in that country. Once assured of the quality, Fender purchased from Russia the largest order of vacuum tubes ever.
- Famous Stratocaster fans include Jimi Hendrix, Eric Clapton, Jeff Beck, Stevie Ray Vaughan, Bonnie Raitt and Richie Sambora.

— BLUES FOUNDATION HALL OF FAME — INDUCTEES FOR ALBUMS

Year	Recipient	Title
2003	Junior Wells	*It's My Life, Baby!*
2002	BB King	*Live From Cook County Jail*
2001	Muddy Waters	*The Complete Plantation Recordings* (MCA/Chess)
2000	'Mississippi' Fred McDowell	*Mississippi Delta Blues*
1999	Junior Wells	*Blues Hit Big Town*
1998	Albert King	*I'll Play The Blues For You*
1997	Bobby 'Blue' Bland	*Two Steps From The Blues*
1997	The Paul Butterfield Blues Band (Jerome Arnold, Elvin Bishop, Michael Bloomfield, Paul Butterfield, Sam Lay, Mark Naftalin)	*The Paul Butterfield Blues Band*
1996	Hound Dog Taylor And The Houserockers (Ted Harvey, Brewer Phillips, Hound Dog Taylor)	*Hound Dog Taylor And The Houserockers*
1995	Big Joe Turner	*Boss Of The Blues*
1995	Otis Spann	*Otis Spann Is The Blues*
1994	T-Bone Walker	*The Complete T-Bone Walker 1940–1954*
1994	Wynonie Harris	
1993	Jimmy Rogers	*Chicago Bound*
1992	Bukka White	*Parchman Farm*
1992	Son House	*Father Of Folk Blues*
1992	Champion Jack Dupree	*Blues From The Gutter*
1992	Robert Johnson	The Complete Recordings

— BLUES FOUNDATION HALL OF FAME — INDUCTEES FOR ALBUMS (CONTINUED)

1991	Little Walter	*The Best Of Little Walter*
1991	Various Artists	*Chicago, The Blues Today*
1991	Jimmy Rogers	*Chicago Bound*
1991	Muddy Waters	*Can't Get No Grindin'*
1991	Muddy Waters	*The Muddy Waters Box Set*
1990	Magic Sam	*Black Magic*
1990	Skip James	*The Complete 1931 Session*
1990	Willie Dixon	*The Chess Box*
1988	Little Walter	*Boss Blues Harmonica*
1988	Elmore James	*The Original Flair And Meteor Sides*
1988	Muddy Waters	*Down On Stovall's Plantation*
1988	Muddy Waters	*The Chess Box*
1988	Bessie Smith	*The World's Greatest Blues Singer*
1988	Otis Rush	*Right Place, Wrong Time*
1988	Robert Nighthawk	*Live On Maxwell Street*
1988	Albert Collins/Robert Cray/Johnny Copeland	*Showdown*
1987	Willie Dixon	*I Am The Blues*
1987	Leroy Carr	*Blues Before Sunrise*
1986	Albert King	*Live Wire*
1986	Freddie King	*Hideaway*
1986	Albert Collins	*Ice Pickin'*
1986	Bobby 'Blue' Bland	*The Best Of Bobby Bland*
1985	Albert King	*Born Under A Bad Sign*
1985	Howlin' Wolf	*Rocking Chair Album*
1985	Howlin' Wolf	*Chester Burnett, AKA Howlin' Wolf*

1984	Muddy Waters	*The Best Of Muddy Waters* and *McKinley Morganfield, AKA Muddy Waters*
1984	Junior Wells	*Hoodoo Man Blues*
1983	Charlie Patton	*Founder Of The Delta Blues*
1983	Little Walter	*Boss Blues Harmonica*
1982	B.B. King	*Live At The Regal*
1980	Robert Johnson	*King Of The Delta Blues Singers, Vol 1 & 2*
1980	Magic Sam	*West Side Soul*

— A SELECTION OF DJ SCRATCHES —

Forward And Backward Scratches
Baby Scratch
Chop/Jab/Stab Scratch
Rub Scratch
Tear Scratch
Echo Fade Scratch
Transform Scratch
Flare Scratch
Orbit Scratch
Crab Scratch
Twiddle Scratch
Chirp Scratch
Scribble Scratch
Tweak Scratch
Bubble Scratch
Zig-Zag Scratch

— ORIGINAL HEAVY (METAL) WEIGHTS —

Led Zeppelin • Deep Purple • Black Sabbath
Iron Maiden • Motörhead • Metallica
Alice Cooper • Judas Priest • Thin Lizzy • KISS

THE MOTHER'S DAY MIXTAPE
— (MUSIC TO KEEP YOUR MOMMA SWEET TO) —

'Mother Superior' – The Beatles
'Mother' – Pink Floyd
'Send A Picture Of Mother' – Johnny Cash
'Mom And Dad' – Cub
'Honour Your Mother And Your Father' – Desmond Dekker
'Mama Tried' – Merle Haggard
'I'll Always Love My Momma' – The O'Jays
'A Vision Of Mother' – The Osborne Brothers
'Dear Mama' – Tupac
'Oh Mother Of Mine' – The Temptations
'Mother' – John Lennon
'Mama' – The Spice Girls
'Mother, Mother' – Tracy Bonham
'Cleaning Out My Closet (I'm Sorry Mama)' – Eminem

— FAMOUS LONDON MUSIC HALLS —

*The first music halls appeared in London after 1843, when the Theatre Act of that year declared that establishments would be licensed only if they were operated as theatres. Venues began to provide different types of entertainment, from comedy and song to singers, acrobats and magicians. By 1875 there were over 300 music halls in London, with hundreds more scattered across the British Isles.

Alhambra Theatre
Coal Hole, Strand
Canterbury Music Hall
Charing Cross Theatre
Evan's Supper Rooms
Elephant And Castle Theatre
Foresters Music Hall
Globe Theatre
London Hippodrome
Hoxton Varieties
London Pavilion Theatre
Lyceum Theatre

The Marylebone
Olympic Theatre
Oxford Music Hall
Playhouse
Prince Of Wales Theatre
Royal Standard Music Hall
Tivoli Theatre
Victoria Palace
Windmill Theatre

— DES ODEUR: A SCALE OF PERFUMES —

In 1865, Parisian perfume manufacturer Charles Piesse devised a fragrance classification system that related specific fragrances to specific music notes, and the mixing of perfume odours to corresponding musical chords. His system spanned six and a half octaves, with patchouli at the lowest C to civet at the highest F. In the 1920s, William Poucher continued the theme with the 'Fragrance Pyramid', whereby oils and perfumes are divided into top, middle and bass notes. Poucher's classification is still used today in professions such as perfumery and aromatherapy.

— THE SUZUKI METHOD —

Dr Shinichi Suzuki (1898–1998) was the son of Japan's first and largest violin manufacturer. After observing how easily young children learnt to speak their mother tongue through listening, imitation and repetition, he concluded that children could also learn music the same way. His method takes a 'character first, ability second' approach, so that the teaching of notation is delayed until an adequate grounding in playing skills has been established. Suzuki called his idea 'Talent Education' and established a school in Matsumoto. Today there are over 8,000 Suzuki teachers worldwide and more than 250,000 children learning by the Suzuki Method.

— TEMPO DYNAMICS —

Name	Meaning
Largo	Very slowly, stately
Larghetto	Slowly, but not as slow as largo
Lento	Slowly
Adagio	Slowly, leisurely
Andante	Moving gently, flowing
Andantino	A bit faster than andante
Moderato	Moderate
Allegretto	Moderately fast
Allegro	Fast, cheerful
Vivace	Lively
Presto	Fast
Prestissimo	Very fast

— THE TARANTELLA DANCE —

The Tarantella dance originated in the Middle Ages in Magna Grecia, an area that included North Africa, Greece and Southern Italy. The dance has its roots in the myth of Arachne, whereby a princess transforms into a spider. Tarantulas were often found by female field workers, who developed the dancing ritual in the belief that it would cure tarantismo – the disease that was said to be caused by tarantula bites. Around the time of the summer solstice, those who suffered from the bites – the tarantate – would meet in a secret place for three days and three nights of dancing, whipping themselves into an ecstatic trance of liberation and purification until they were healed.

— TEREZIN —

Terezin was an 18th-century fort that was converted into a concentration camp by the Nazis during World War II. The place was flaunted as a haven for Jewish people and was the subject of a documentary called *Hitler Builds A Town For The Jews*. Notable musicians, writers, artists and leaders were sent there for 'safer' keeping than was to be afforded elsewhere in Hitler's quest to stave off any uprisings or objections around the so-called civilised world. Terezin had its own orchestra and a jazz band (The Ghetto Swingers). A number of distinguished composers created works at Terezin, including *Brundibar*, or *The*

Bumble Bee (a children's operetta), and a number of chamber compositions. The most famous was Viktor Ullmann's *The Emperor Of Atlantis*, which was banned by authorities while in rehearsal. Other composers included Pavel Haas, Gideo Klein and Hans Krasa. The camp was liberated by the Red Cross in 1945. Of the 139,654 people who were sent to Terezin, only 17,320 survived.

— PERSONNEL ON *KIND OF BLUE* —

*Recorded in 1959, Miles Davis's *Kind Of Blue* is considered be one of the greatest and most influential jazz albums of all time. An overt revolt against the incessant chord changes associated with the bebop and cool movements, it ushered in the modal jazz era and brought together the following musicians, most of whom are now legendary:

Miles Davis – *Trumpet*
John Coltrane – *Tenor Saxophone*
Julian 'Cannonball' Adderley – *Alto Saxophone*
Bill Evans – *Piano*
Wynton Kelly – *Piano*
Paul Chambers – *Bass*
Jimmy Cobb – *Drums*

— ACCORDION PLAYERS IN CHINA (BY PROVINCE) —

*There are more accordion players in China than anywhere else in the world. The country currently has over 300,000 accordion students, a number which is increasing by 20 per cent each year.

Province	No. Of Players
Hebei	80,000
Jiangsu	60,000
Liaoning	20,000
Sichuan	20,000
Fujian	20,000
Guangdong	20,000
Heilongjiang	10,000
Hubei	10,000
Hunan	10,000
Shanxi	10,000

— PROMINENT AFRICAN MUSIC STYLES —

Marabi (South Africa) • Jit • (Zimbabwe) • Afrobeat (Nigeria) • Apala (Nigeria) • Apala (Nigeria) • Kwassa Kwassa (Zaire) • Jive (South Africa) • Makossa (Cameroon) • Marrabenta (Mozambique) • Fuji (Nigeria) • Mbalax (Senegal) • Morna (Cape Verde) • Iscathamiya (South Africa) • Palm Wine (Sierra Leone) • Rai (Algeria) • Wassoulou (Mali) • Mbaqanga (South Africa) • Benga (Kenya) • Gnawa (Morocco) • Highlife (Ghana) • Chimurenga (Zimbabwe) • Kwela (South Africa) • Juju (Nigeria)

— SCARED STARS —

Fear Of Flying – Aretha Franklin, David Bowie, Cher, Loretta Lynn
Fear Of Cows – Lyle Lovett
Fear Of Snakes – Johnny Cash
Fear Of Germs – Michael Jackson
Fear Of Elevators – Dean Martin
Fear Of Performance (Stage Fright) – Barbra Streisand, Donny Osmond, Carly Simon
Fear Of Heights – Brian Littrell (Backstreet Boys)
Fear Of Clowns – P Diddy
Anxiety Disorders – David Bowie, Naomi Judd, Deanna Carter, Sheryl Crow, Eric Clapton, Ray Charles, Bonnie Raitt

— MINSTRELRY —

One of the originators of the Minstrel Shows in the USA (ie shows where white performers rubbed burnt cork on their faces to imitate African-Americans) was Thomas Dartmouth 'Daddy' Rice (1808–1860), who developed a song-and-dance routine in which he impersonated an old, crippled black slave called Jim Crow, whom he had observed entertaining his fellow workers in a stable. His routine achieved immediate popularity, and Rice became successful in the US and Great Britain, where he introduced it in 1836. One of the first full minstrel groups were The Virginia Minstrels, who devised a programme of singing and dancing in blackface to the accompaniment of bone castanets, fiddles, banjos and tambourines. Minstrelry was at its height between 1850 and 1870, after which the popularity of the style declined rapidly. By 1919, only three troupes remained in the US.

— CHICAGO HOUSE PIONEERS —

*House music was born from a merging of disco and the music of avant-garde electronic bands like Kraftwerk and The Yellow Magic Orchestra. The genre's name was taken from Chicago club the Warehouse, where the music was played. The following Chicago-based DJs and producers played a seminal role in spawning the house-music revolution.

Jesse Saunders
Adonis
Farley 'Jackmaster' Funk
Ron Hardy
Frankie Knuckles
Larry Heard
Steve Hurley
Robert Owens
DJ Pierre
Vince Lawrence
Byron Burke
Ralphi Rosario
Ten City

— DROPLIFTING —

The art of sneaking CDs of your own music onto shelves at retail music stores.

— SONGS DEEMED UNSUITABLE TO PLAY ON — BBC RADIO DURING THE GULF CRISIS

Abba 'Waterloo'
A-Ha 'Hunting High And Low'
The Animals 'We Got To Get Out Of This Place'
Arrival 'I Will Survive'
The Bangles 'Walk Like An Egyptian'
Big Country 'Fields Of Fire'
The Boomtown Rats 'I Don't Like Mondays'
Eric Clapton 'I Shot The Sheriff'
Phil Collins 'In The Air Tonight'
Dire Straits 'Brothers In Arms'
Duran Duran 'View To A Kill'
Roberta Flack 'Killing Me Softly'
Frankie Goes To Hollywood 'Two Tribes'
Johnny Hates Jazz 'I Don't Want To Be A Hero'
John Lennon 'Give Peace A Chance'
Jona Louis 'Stop The Cavalry'
M*A*S*H 'Suicide Is Painless'
Billy Ocean 'When The Going Gets Tough'
Queen 'Flash'
BA Robertson 'Bang Bang'
The Specials 'Ghost Town'
Edwin Starr 'War'
Cat Stevens 'I'm Gonna Get Me A Gun'
Tears For Fears 'Everybody Wants To Rule The World'

— THE FLORENTINE CAMERATA —

The beginnings of opera can be traced back to Jacopo Peri, Giulio Caccini and Emilio de' Cavalieri, aka the Florentine Camerata. These three men were employed at the Grand-Ducal court in Florence and fought for the revival of Ancient Greek drama, calling especially for words to be placed in a musical setting. The first surviving opera is considered to be Peri's *Euridice*, written in 1600. This opera and other works by the Florentine Camerata laid the foundation upon which Monteverdi, the first great opera composer, built his own works. A 'camerata' today refers to a musical group, instrumental or choral of virtually any size.

— TEN CLASSIC LEE 'SCRATCH' PERRY PRODUCTIONS —

'Party Time' – The Heptones – 1977
'Police And Thieves' – Junior Murvin – 1977
'Open The Gate' – Watty Burnett – 1976
'Don't Blame It On I' – The Congos 1978
'I Chase The Devil' – Max Romeo – 1976
'Congoman' – The Congos -1977
'Groovy Situation' – Keith Rowe – 1977
'Soul Fire' – Lee Perry – 1978
'Small Axe' – The Wailers – 1970

— A SELECTION OF EUROPEAN FOLK DANCES —

Black Nag – *English*
Bourée Droite – *French*
Cocek-Durdevan – *Bulgarian*
De'il Amang the Tailors – *Scottish*
Devetorka (Nishka Banja) – *Serbian*
Dimna Juda Mamo – *Macedonian*
Erev Ba – *Israeli*
Fado Blanquita – *Spanish*
Familie Sekstur – *Danish*
Gerankina – *Greek*
Hora Czardeska – *Polish*
Juice of the Barley – *English*
Karapyet – *Russian*
Krici, Krici Ticek – *Croatian*
La Bastringue – *French-Canadian*
Lukket Reinlander – *Norwegian*
Opsa – *Bulgarian*
Queen's Jig – *English*
Ugros – *Hungarian*
Wild Geese Jig – *Scottish*

— FIVE DRUMMERS WHO SING —

Phil Collins (Genesis)
Don Henley (The Eagles)
Ringo Starr (The Beatles)
Karen Carpenter (The Carpenters)
Mickey Dolenz (The Monkees)

— THE ZEN MIX TAPE (MUSIC TO MEDITATE TO) —

*Many of the following recordings are conceptual pieces and contain little or no music. Do not ask for a refund as you'll look silly.

Mike Batt, 'A Minute's Silence'	2002
John Cage, '4' 33"'	1952
Steve Reich, 'Pendulum Music'	1968
Matmos, 'Always Three Words'	1998
John Cage, 'Silent Prayer'	1949
Reynols, 'Blank Tapes'	1999
Psychodrama's, 'No Tape'	1984
Psychodrama, 'The Wit And Wisdom of Ronald Reagan'	1980
Columbia Records, 'Three Minutes Of Silence' (to combat the 'noisy' jukebox boom)	1953

— PATTING JUBA —

In 1739, slaves on a plantation in South Carolina attempted to escape by killing two guards and fleeing towards Florida. They marched to the beat of two drums, signalling to other slaves to join them and killing whites who interfered. They were eventually stopped by the militia at the Stono River. This incident provoked the authorities to outlaw the use of drums, which in turn inspired the slaves to come up with new ways to make rhythms. They did this mainly by using their own bodies as drums, ie hand clapping and body and thigh slapping. This became known as 'patting Juba' and is considered the forerunner of popular 20th-century dance styles such as tap dancing and the charleston.

— TECHNICS DMC DJ COMPETITION WINNERS —

1986 DJ Cheese (USA)
1987 Chad Jackson (UK)
1988 Cash Money (USA)
1989 Cutmaster Swift (UK)
1990 DJ David Fascher (Germany)
1991 DJ David Fascher (Germany)
1992 Rock Steady DJs (USA)
1993 The Dream Team (USA)
1994 Roc Raida (USA)
1995 Roc Raida (USA)
1996 DJ Noize (Denmark)
1997 A Trak (Canada)
1998 DJ Craze (USA)
1999 DJ Craze (USA)
2000 DJ Craze (USA)
2001 Plus One (UK)
2002 Kentaro (Japan)

— TEN THINGS YOU POSSIBLY DIDN'T KNOW — ABOUT...THE SEX PISTOLS

- The Sex Pistols were formerly known as The Swankers.
- Most of the musical equipment the band started with was shoplifted by Paul Cook and Steve Jones.
- The Sex Pistols lasted ten days on the A&M record label before the company pulled out.
- Bass player Sid Vicious didn't know how to play the instrument when he joined the band in 1977.
- They released only one actual album, *Never Mind The Bollocks, Here's The Sex Pistols*.
- Sid Vicious's mother scattered his ashes throughout Heathrow Airport.
- John Lydon was called 'Johnny Rotten' because Malcom McLaren noted the rotten state of his teeth.
- The only open (non-bar) chord The Sex Pistols ever played was a G.

— TEN THINGS YOU POSSIBLY DIDN'T KNOW — ABOUT...THE SEX PISTOLS (CONTINUED)

- Sid Vicious once settled an argument with a trucker in a diner by slicing open his own wrist with a knife.
- The Sex Pistols got their first gig in November 1975 at a suburban London art school. Someone pulled the plug after ten minutes.

— INSTRUMENTS FOR MODERN BALINESE GAMELAN — (GONG KEBYAR)

Modern gamelan Bali (*gong kebyar*) began in the early parts of the 20th century. Kebyar ('sudden outburst') was influenced by the many gamelan traditions of Bali and Java, but also by the influence of Western music introduced by the Dutch. The resulting new instrumentation provided great dynamic range in both frequency and volume and extensive harmonic colouring. In gong kebyar, many of the instruments are paired. Each member of a pair is tuned slightly differently in order to create the shimmering sound that is characteristic of Gamelan Bali.

Ugal • Jegogan • Jublag • Kantil • Pemade Reyong Gongs • Kendhang • Kempli • Ceng-Ceng and Trompong.

— GALILEO GALILEI: THE FATHER OF ACOUSTICS —

Galileo Galilei (1564–1642) became known as the father of acoustics following his seminal work *Mathematical Discourses Concerning Two New Sciences* (published in 1638). In the book, Galileo elevated the study of vibrations and the correlation between pitch and frequency of the sound source to scientific standards. His work contained the most lucid statement and discussion given up until then of the frequency equivalence, and revealed the general principles behind sympathetic vibrations, or resonance, and the correspondence between the frequency of vibrations and the length of a pendulum. Galileo's interest in sound was inspired in part by his father, who was a mathematician, musician and composer.

— JUKEBOX FACTS —

- The word *jukebox* is taken from *jook*, an old African-American term meaning 'to dance' (amongst other things).
- The first public appearance of a Nickel In The Slot phonograph machine was in 1889, when Louis Glass and William S Arnold placed a coin-operated Edison cylinder phonograph in the Palais Royale Saloon in San Francisco.
- The Wurlitzer family started buying and selling musical items in Saxony as far back as 1659.
- The first Wurlitzer jukebox was called 'the Debutante'.
- The most popular jukebox of all time is the Wurlitzer model 1015, known colloquially as 'the Bubbler'.
- The name Rock-Ola is derived from the name of the company's founder, David C Rockola.
- Seeburg's 1928 Audiophone was one of the first multi-select jukeboxes.
- The first jukebox to play 45rpm records was the M100B, made by Seeburg in 1950.
- When Queen Mary made her maiden voyage from New York City in 1936, David C Rockola delivered one of his 12-Selecter Jukeboxes to her decks. The headline read: 'The Queen Will Have Music Wherever She Goes'.
- By the late 1930s, Wurlitzer was producing over 45,000 jukeboxes per year.
- CD jukeboxes started to be manufactured in 1987.

— TABLA BOL —

Tabla bol is the individual sound produced by striking various parts of the dayan and the bayan, or a combination of the two drums. Tabla bol makes up the vocabulary of the tabla, and bols may be voiced or played on the tabla. Learning the bols can be compared to learning the alphabet, since bols form words and sentences that can be weaved into paragraphs and stories. As with language dialects, terminology pronunciations for the bol vary from region to region though the structure remains the same.

— SACRED BATA DRUMS —

The sacred bata drums of Yorubaland are used predominantly for the worship of Shangó, the deified historical leader of Oyó and God of thunder and lightning. The drums have religious rituals surrounding their construction which determine who can touch them, how to prepare to play them and how to care for them. The spiritual force and mystery placed within the drum when it is made sacred, or consecrated, is called *añá* or *ayán*. Añá is also referred to as an *orisha*, or deity. A drummer may be initiated into añá through certain religious rituals practiced mostly in Cuba (and Nigeria) and receives the spiritual force needed to play the drums correctly to bring the orishas down to a ceremony to possess the devotees. An uninitiated person may not touch the drums and they are not allowed to touch the ground.

— SOME POTENTIALLY INTERESTING FACTS — ABOUT BAGPIPES

- Bagpipes are not unique to Scotland. There are over 40 types of bagpipe in the world, including the Picardy, the Shepherd's, the Goatherd's, the Uillean (Irish), and the Galician.
- There are five main parts to a bagpipe: a blowpipe, three drones and a chanter.
- A set of Highland warpipes typically weighs between 5lbs and 16lbs.
- The bag is generally made from cured sheepskin.
- The average kilt consists of an average of 18 square yards of material and contains over 250 pleats.
- 'Black lung' is a disease pipers used to suffer from. It was caused by inhaling the fungus that grows inside the bag.
- Pipers were often also clan doctors. During battles, the piper would continue his music so that the wounded would know which way to go.

- The bagpipes have only nine notes. They are not set in the usual Western major or minor scales but in the ancient Lydian/Mixolydian modal system.
- Most of the written music for the bagpipe can be traced to the MacCrimmons, the greatest family of pipers ever known.
- Biblical mention is made of the bagpipe in Genesis and in the third chapter of Daniel, where the 'symphonia' in Nebuchadnezzar's band is believed to have been a bagpipe.
- On the eighth day, God created Pipers!
- After the Uprising of 1745, the playing of the pipes was forbidden in Scotland, but it was kept alive in secret, and once the ban was lifted, bagpipe music began to flourish.
- In the movie *Braveheart* (1995), the previews show a piper on a hillside with the great highland bagpipes in the soundtrack. The bagpipes shown on the screen are of the modern variety – 400 years ahead of their time.

— BLACK POWER ANTHEMS —

Aretha Franklin, 'Respect', 1967
James Brown, 'Say It Loud (I'm Black And I'm Proud)', 1969
Curtis Mayfield And The Impressions, 'Keep On Pushing', 1964
Marvin Gaye, 'You're The Man', 1972
Gil Scott-Heron, 'The Revolution Will Not Be Televised', 1974
Main Ingredient, 'Black Seeds Keep On Growing', 1971
Bob Marley And The Wailers, 'Get Up, Stand Up', 1973
Funkadelic, 'One Nation Under The Groove', 1978
Bob Marley, 'Concrete Jungle', 1972
Public Enemy, 'Don't Believe The Hype', 1988
Deniece Williams, 'Black Butterfly', 1984
Public Enemy, 'Fight The Power', 1990
X Clan, 'Raise The Flag', 1990
Fred Hammond, 'No Weapon', 1996
Public Enemy, 'Brothers Gonna Work It Out', 1990
Mos' Def, 'Umi Says', 2002

— TOP TEN RADIO FORMATS IN THE USA —

* There are twice as many country-music stations in the US as any other format.

(1) Country
(2) News/Talk
(3) Oldies
(4) Adult Contemporary
(5) Hispanic
(6) Adult Standards
(7) Top 40
(8) Soft Adult Contemporary
(9) Religion (Teaching, Variety)
(10) Classic Rock

— SPECIALIST ELECTRONIC GENRES —

Illbient	Epic Trance	Future Hard House
Happy House	Oriental House	Sombient
Intelligent Dance Music	Happycore	Terrorcore
Deathcore	Partycore	Big Room Electro
Space Funk	Hardbag	Handbag
Breakbeat Ballad	Future Jungle	Gabbercore
Acid Gabba	Breakstep	Tripsco
Dhol And Bass	Ethno House	Handbag Jungle
Speed Garage		

— VIBRATO —

A musical effect where the pitch of a note is wavered quickly and repeatedly over a small distance for the duration of that note. The effect is intended to add warmth to a note and is used in particular by wind players, string players and singers. With regard to singers, the louder the note, the more pronounced the vibrato tends to be. The oscillation can become so wide that the hearer may be left in doubt as to just which note is being aimed for. A helpful side-effect is that it can help to disguise poor tuning.

— A SELECTION OF SINGING COWBOY MOVIES —

In My Old Arizona (Warner Baxter) 1929
Rhythm On The Range (Bing Crosby) 1936
Sing, Cowboy, Sing (Tex Ritter) 1937
A Gay Ranchero (Roy Rogers) 1947
Cowboy's Heaven (Gene Autry) 1933
Come On Boys, We're Riding Into Town (Ray Whitely) 1938
That's What I Like About The West (Tex Williams) 1949
Texas Toni Lee (Pee Wee King) 1946
Ridin' Down To Santa Fé (Merle Travis) 1945

— THE SPEED OF SOUND —

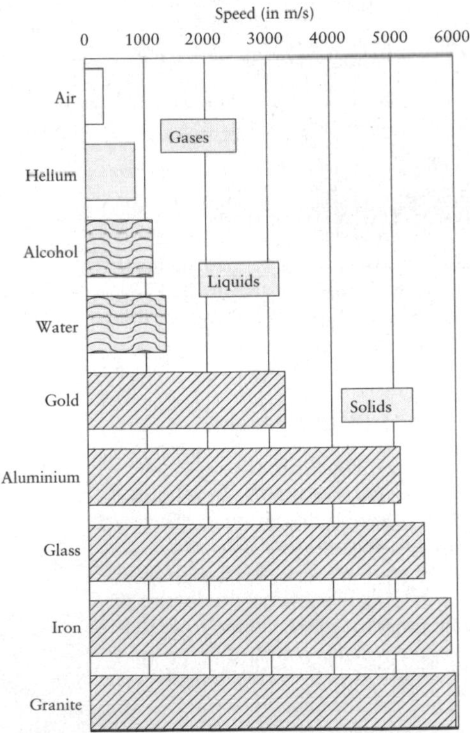

— DUB CONQUERERS —

Dub was pioneered in Jamaica, principally by producers King Tubby and Lee Perry, both of whom used their studio mixing desks as instruments. Their music is characterised by a stripped-down sound that reduces reggae music to its 'drum and bass' skeleton, leaving only a slight residue of other instruments, and adding liberal amounts of effects such as echo and reverb.

King Tubby
Lee Scratch Perry
Bunny Lee
Overton 'Scientist' Brown
Adrian Sherwood
Mad Professor
Dub Syndicate
Augustus Pablo
Yabby You
Jah Shaka
'Prince' Philip Smart

— THE LONGEST RENDERING OF — A NATIONAL ANTHEM

'God Save The King' was performed by a German military band on the platform of Rathenau railway station in Brandenburg on 9 February 1909. Since King Edward VII was struggling inside the train to get into his German field-marshal uniform, the band had to play the anthem 17 times.

— LONGEST RAP ALIAS —

Dr Wolfgang Von Bushwickinthe Barbarian Mother Funky Stay High Dollar Billster – aka 'Bushwick Bill'.

— THE FIRST POP VIDEO —

Queen, 'Bohemian Rhapsody', 1975.

— JAZZ CHAT —

Blow The playing of any jazz instrument (whether blown or not).
Blue notes The flatted third and seventh, which create the blues scale.
Boogie-woogie Piano blues style.
Bop Generic term for '40s styles of modern jazz (originally known as bebop or rebop).
Bug To annoy
Cat Musician.
Chase Alternation of solos by two or more musicians.
Chip Girl.
Chops Lips.
Clambake An improvised session which doesn't come off.
Cool Restrained.
Cut or cut out To leave, to depart; or to defeat a soloist or band in a competition.
Dad or daddy-o A form of address amongst friends.
Dig To understand.
Dog tune A song of questionable quality.
Fake To improvise.
Hip Initiated, knowing.
Horn Any instrument (not just the brass).
Icky One who does not dig.
Lick A phrase or a solo.
Torch song Ballad of unrequited love.
Zoot Exaggerated clothing.

— THE LONGEST SONG TITLE IN THE WORLD —

'I'm A Cranky Old Yank In A Clanky Old Tank On The Streets Of Yokohama With My Honolulu Mama Doin' Those Beat-o, Beat-o Flat-On-My-Seat-o, Hirohito Blues' – Hoagy Carmichael, 1943.

— BANDS NAMED AFTER ANIMALS —

The Animals
The Monkees
Echo And The Bunnymen
Skunk Anansie
The Eagles
The Byrds
Whitesnake
Def Leppard
The Housemartins
The Turtles
The Blow Monkeys
Steppenwolf
The Yardbirds
A Flock Of Seagulls
The Beatles
The Crickets
The Black Crows
Lamb
Seal
Crazy Horse
The Boomtown Rats
The Soup Dragons
The Stray Cats
Buffalo Springfield
Pigbag
Camel
Iron Butterfly
The Bees
The Fabulous Poodles
T Rex

— LONGEST CAREER FOR AN AFRICAN — RECORDING ARTIST

Nigerian-born Fela Anikulapo Kuti – aka Fela Kuti – enjoyed a career spanning 37 years, from 1960 until he died, in 1997. His last recording was made in 1992.

— SOME WELL-KNOWN CHOREOGRAPHERS —

Martha Graham
Lew Christensen
Agnes De Mille
Katherine Dunham
Bob Fosse, American
Twyla Tharp
Mikhail Fokine
Vaslaw Nijinski
Merce Cunningham
Sergei Diaghilev
Paul Taylor
Georges Balanchine
Marius Petipa
Pina Bausch
Rudolph Laba
William Forsythe
Lincoln Kirstein
Pierre Beauchamps
Leonid Massine
Antony Tudor
Paula Abdul

— CONCERT PERFORMED IN MOST CONTINENTS — IN 24 HOURS

On 23 October 1995, Def Leppard played in Africa, Europe and North America. Each of the concerts lasted for at least one hour and was attended by 200 or more people. The first gig started at 12:23am in Morocco. The band then flew to London for the second concert and finished in Vancouver, Canada, at 11:33pm on the same day.

— MOST SIBLINGS IN ONE GROUP —

The Jets, who had one hit with 'Crush On You' in 1987, were comprised of eight brothers and sisters from the Wolfgramm family. They were Leroy, Eddie, Eugene, Haini, Rudy, Kathi, Elizabeth and Moana.

— I GOT RHYTHM —

'Rhythm' is one of the longest English words without vowels.

— FIRST COUNTRY ARTIST TO BE HEARD — IN OUTER SPACE.

Merle Haggard, whose music was played by astronaut Charles Duke on board *Apollo 16* in 1972, almost 60,000 miles from Earth.

— DISCOTHÈQUES —

The term *discothèque* is a composite of the Greek words *doskis* ('disc') and *theke* (container). The first discothèques were in France, which is where the word was invented. During the Nazi occupation of Paris in World War II, jazz bands were driven out of clubs, but the public still wanted entertainment, so the clubs moved into gloomy cellars on left bank of the Seine and installed record players and speakers. When the war was over, some of the live clubs re-opened, but the concept of playing records stayed. The full scope of the discothèque was discovered in America, with seminal '60s venues such as Le Club, L'interdit, Il Mio Club and Shepheards.

— TOP-SELLING ALBUMS OF ALL TIME —

The Eagles – *Greatest Hits 1971–1975* (Elektra) – 28 Million

Michael Jackson – *Thriller* (Epic) – 26 Million

Pink Floyd – *The Wall* (Columbia) – 23 Million

Led Zeppelin – *IV* (Swan Song) – 22 Million

Billy Joel – *Greatest Hits Volumes I And II* – (Columbia) – 21 Million

AC/DC – *Back In Black* (Elektra) /
The Beatles – *The Beatles* (Capitol) /
Shania Twain – *Come On Over* (Mercury Nashville) – 19 Million

Fleetwood Mac – *Rumours* (Warner Bros) – 18 Million

Whitney Houston – *The Bodyguard* (soundtrack, Arista) – 17 Million

Boston – *Boston* (Epic) / Hootie And The Blowfish – *Cracked Rear View* (Atlantic) / Eagles – *Hotel California* (Elektra) / Alanis Morissette – *Jagged Little Pill* (Maverick) / Garth Brooks – *No Fences* (Capitol Nashville) / The Beatles – *The Beatles 1967–1970* (Capitol) – 16 Million

— OLDEST PLAYABLE INSTRUMENT IN THE WORLD —

In 1999 archaeologists uncovered six Chinese bone flutes, the oldest of which is reckoned to be 9,000 years old. The flute is 8.6' long, has seven holes and is made from the leg of a red-crowned crane. It was found at Jiahu, the site of an ancient farming village on the Yellow River flood plain, China.

— THE DRUGS DON'T WORK: MUSICIANS WHO TOOK — THE ROCK 'N' ROLL ROUTE OUT OF LIFE

John Belushi (*The Blues Brothers*) – heroin/cocaine – 1982
Bix Beiderbecke (trumpeter) – alcohol – 1931
Big Maybelle (singer) – heroin – 1971
Steve Clark (Def Leppard) – drugs/alcohol – 1991
Pete Farndon (The Pretenders) – drugs – 1983
Billie Holiday (singer)– drugs/alcohol – 1959
Brian Jones (The Rolling Stones) – 'Death By Misadventure' – 1969
Phil Lynott (Thin Lizzy) – drugs – 1986
Keith Moon (The Who) – prescription drugs – 1978
Jim Morrison (The Doors) – drugs/heart attack – 1971
David Ruffin (The Temptations) – crack cocaine – 1991
Janis Joplin (singer) – heroin – 1970
Sid Vicious (The Sex Pistols) – heroin – 1979
Tim Buckley (singer) – heroin/morphine – 1975.
Bon Scott (AC/DC) – alcohol -1980
Vinnie Taylor (Canned Heat) – drugs – 1974
Brian Epstein (The Beatles' Manager) – drugs – 1967
Fats Waller (singer) – alcohol – 1943
Jimi Hendrix (guitarist) – drugs – 1970

— BACH FAMILY —

The Bachs, a German family of musicians, lived and worked in central Germany (mainly Thuringia) from the 16th century to the 18th. Over 70 Bachs at some time earned their livelihoods through music, representing the most remarkable and consistent concentration of musical talent ever recorded in a single family. Some were fiddlers or town musicians. Others were organists, court musicians, Kantors and Kapellmeisters.

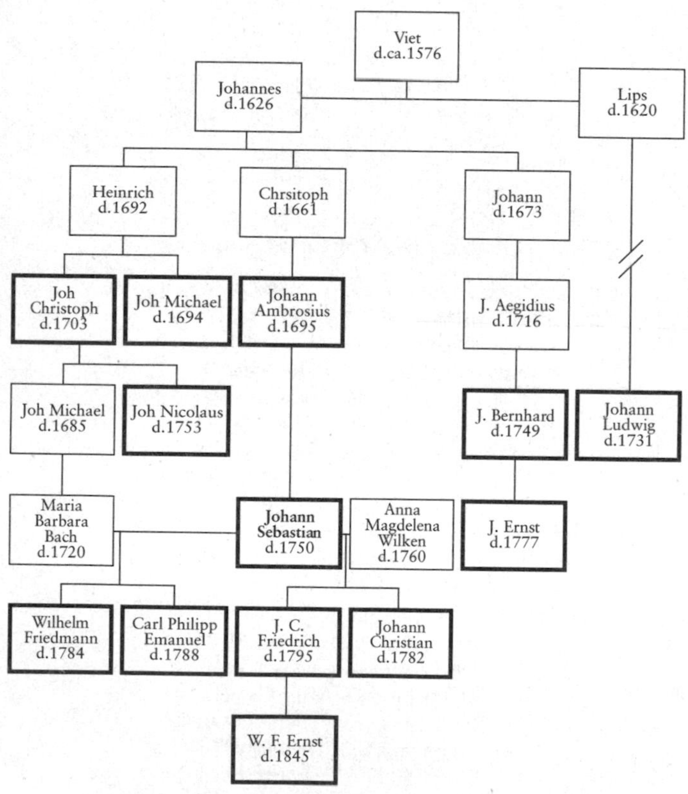

— THE WORLD'S LARGEST DRUM KIT —

Built by American Dan McCourt, a 308-piece drum kit was set up on 6 December 1994 for a show at the Sanctuary nightclub. It took 12 hours for a ten man crew to assemble the kit, which consisted of 153 drums, 77 cymbals, 33 cowbells, 12 hi-hats, 8 tambourines, 6 wood blocks, 3 gongs, 3 bell trees, 2 maracas, 2 triangles, 2 rain sticks, 2 bells, 1 ratchet, 1 set of chimes, 1 xylophone, 1 afuche...and a doorbell.

— THEMES EXPLORED BY ROMANTIC COMPOSERS —

Faraway lands	The past	Dreams
Night	Moonlight	Rivers
Lakes	Forests	Nature
The seasons	Love	Fairy tales
The supernatural	Magic	Tragic love
Individualism	National heritage	Adultery
Death	Suffering	Hope

— THEIR FORMER BANDS —

Marc Almond – Soft Cell
Richard Ashcroft – The Verve
Phil Bailey – Earth, Wind And Fire
Gary Barlow – Take That
Boy George – Bow Wow Wow/Culture Club
Ian Brown – The Stone Roses
Captain Sensible – The Damned
Eric Clapton – The Yardbirds
N'dea Davenport – The Brand New Heavies
Bryan Ferry – Roxy Music
Eazy-E – NWA
Everlast – House Of Pain
Phil Collins – Genesis
Peter Gabriel – Genesis
David Bryne – Talking Heads
Roddy Frame – Aztec Camera
Nick Heyward – Haircut 100
Lauryn Hill – The Fugees
Edwyn Collins – Orange Juice
Peter Frampon – The Herd/Humble Pie
Ice Cube – NWA

— THEIR FORMER BANDS (CONTINUED) —

Billy Idol – Generation X
Ronan Keating – Boyzone
Annie Lennox – The Tourists/The Eurythmics
George Michael – Wham!
Michael MacDonald – The Doobie Brothers
Van Morrisson – Them
Alison Moyet – Yazoo
Phil Lynott – Thin Lizzy
Q-Tip – A Tribe Called Quest
Lionel Richie – The Commodores
Diana Ross – The Supremes
Shaun Ryder – The Happy Mondays/Black Grape
Feargal Sharkey – The Undertones
Sisqo – Dru Hill
Heather Small – M People
Jimmy Somerville – Bronski Beat/The Communards
Sonique – S'Express
Rod Stewart – The Faces
Frankie Valli – The Four Seasons
David Sylvian – Japan
Midge Ure – The Rich Kids/Slik/Thin Lizzy/Ultravox
Jody Watley – Shalamar
Paul Weller – The Style Council/The Jam
Robbie Williams – Take That
Jah Wobble – PiL
Steve Winwood – The Spencer Davis Group/Traffic

— TINNITUS —

Tinnitus is a condition where an individual hears noise or sound either emanating from the ear or from inside the head as opposed to an external source. It is commonly caused by prolonged exposure to loud sound and is usually incurable. It is thought to be produced by a spontaneous firing of the hair cells in the organ of corti, the part of the inner ear which is excited by the bulging of the basilar membrane. The nerve ends connected to the sensory hair cells transmit the excitation in the form of nerve impulses to the brain. According to estimates by the American Tinnitus Association, at least 12 million Americans have tinnitus. Approximately 75 per cent of all people who experience it are not bothered by it, but it is considered intrusive on a daily basis for the remaining 25 per cent.

— CLEFS —

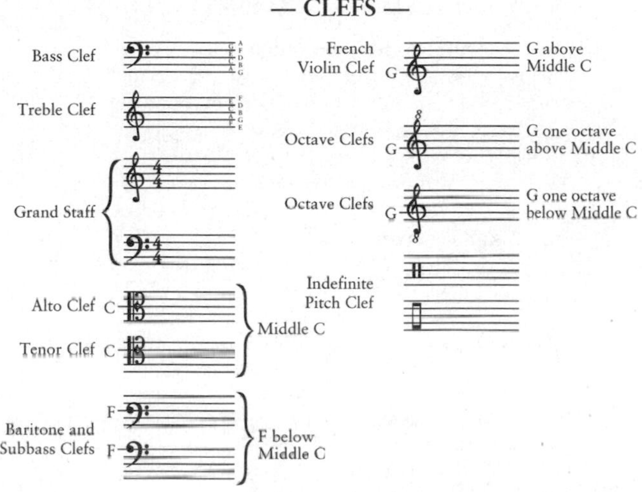

— THE LEGEND OF GLOOMY SUNDAY —

The melancholy song 'Gloomy Sunday' was penned by Hungarian songwriter Reszo Seress in 1932, after he broke up with his girlfriend. The song provided a struggling Seress a deal with a publisher, but a few months after the song was printed, a spate of bizarre suicides occurred – 17 cases in Hungary alone. In all the cases there seemed to be links to the song; either the deceased had been playing the song when they took their life, or they had referred to it in suicide notes, or they were found holding the sheet music to the song. 'Gloomy Sunday' was subsequently banned by Hungarian radio stations, though many more suicides occurred across Europe and America as the song was translated into English and performed by the likes of Billie Holiday and Louis Armstrong. Eventually, other radio stations banned it, including the BBC. It is reported that the composer's girlfriend killed herself shortly after the song was published, and Seress jumped out of a window in 1968.

— HARMONIC CHANT —

Also known as overtone singing, overtoning, toning, harmonic chant, sub-fundamental chant, multiphonic singing, khoomei (throat singing) and vocal fry, harmonic chant is where the constituent parts (overtones or harmonics) are selectively amplified by changing the shape of the resonant cavities of the mouth, larynx and pharynx. For centuries, people in many parts of the world have developed harmonic singing traditions. One of the most well-known areas of harmonic chanting is central Asia, in particular the throat singers of Tuva and Mongolia.

— RADIO FACTS —

- There are almost 45,000 active radio stations in the world.
- On average, FM radio stations broadcast for 20 hours per day, AM stations 16 hours per day, and shortwave stations 12 hours per day.
- There are approximately 300 million hours of radio programming per year.
- There are almost 15,000 radio stations in the United States alone.
- About 84 per cent of US radio stations have music as their primary focus and provide little original content.
- There are currently more than 4,500 streaming radio stations on the Internet.
- The 'call-in' format is the fastest-growing in radio
- Radio reaches 77 per cent of people over the age of 12 every day.
- In 2000, radio's revenue grew to a total of $19.8 billion (£12 billion), up 12 per cent from $17.7 billion (£10 billion) in 1999.
- Radio reaches over 95 per cent of consumers weekly.

— THE WORLDS BEST-SELLING INSTRUMENT —

The Harmonica

**By law, every child in Belgium must take Harmonica lessons at primary school.*

— MUSICAL INJURIES —

Injury	Cause	Symptoms
Chronic lip fatigue	Extensive use of lips	Stiff 'cardboard' lips, bruising, swelling
Carpal tunnel syndrome	Repetitive finger use	Tingling, numbness of the thumb, index and middle fingers
Cubital tunnel syndrome	Repetitive finger use	Pain in elbow, forearm and fingers
Trigger finger	Overuse of finger tendons	Paralysis of finger in fixed position.

— INDEX —

THE A-Z OF RECORD LABELS (SECOND EDITION)

Brian Southall

Foreword by Chris Wright

Since the earliest music companies began, more than 110 years ago, many record labels have come and gone, been taken over or merged. Some have been owned by retailers, DJs, agents or managers, others by artists or vast media, electronics and film companies. From classical to soul, jazz to rock, folk to rap, every record label has its own successes, its own agenda and its own story.

From the dedicated and extraordinary people who founded them, and the corporations who backed them, acquired them or even closed them down, to the artists who brought them fame and fortune, this fully updated edition of the bestselling **The A-Z Of Record Labels** explores the colourful history of one of the most important aspects of popular music.

1 86074 492 3 | £7.99 | $10.95